For Alfie,
born 1 December 2018

# Never leave the dog behind

Our love of dogs and mountains

Helen Mort

Vertebrate Publishing, Sheffield
www.v-publishing.co.uk

# Never leave the dog behind
## Helen Mort

First published in 2020 by Vertebrate Publishing.
This paperback edition first published in 2021 by Vertebrate Publishing.

 Vertebrate Publishing
Omega Court, 352 Cemetery Road, Sheffield S11 8FT, United Kingdom.
www.v-publishing.co.uk

Front cover: Helen and Scout on Higgar Tor. Photo copyright © John Houlihan 2020.
Back cover: Wilbur at the top of Doctor's Gate. Photo copyright © Jon Barton.

Helen Mort has asserted her rights under the Copyright, Designs
and Patents Act 1988 to be identified as author of this work.

This book is a work of non-fiction. The author has stated to the publishers that, except in
such minor respects not affecting the substantial accuracy of the work, the contents of the book are true.

A CIP catalogue record for this book is available from the British Library.

ISBN: 978-1-839810-38-1 (Paperback)
ISBN: 978-1-912560-89-9 (Ebook)

10 9 8 7 6 5 4 3 2 1

Every effort has been made to obtain the necessary permissions with reference to copyright material,
both illustrative and quoted. We apologise for any omissions in this respect and will be pleased to make
the appropriate acknowledgements in any future edition.

 Cover design by Jane Beagley, Vertebrate Publishing.
Production by Cameron Bonser, Vertebrate Publishing.
www.v-publishing.co.uk

Vertebrate Publishing is committed to printing on paper from sustainable sources.

Printed and bound in Great Britain by Clays Ltd, Elcograf S.p.A.

# Contents

# Introduction

July 1805. A Cumbrian shepherd stands to rest, hands on his back, his breathing ragged, beside the paw-shaped expanse of Red Tarn, high on the eastern flank of Helvellyn. Glancing up towards Striding Edge and Catstye Cam, he's distracted by a high, excited yapping. The wind carries the sound to him before he sees the source of it. A small dog – perhaps a spaniel – is running in rings and flattening itself against the ground. He moves towards it. The dog is circling a mound of rags. On closer inspection, he can see that they are clothes. A good jacket. Then he starts abruptly, shivers: beside the jacket lies a skeleton, too long, too large to be the body of a sheep. A gold watch glints in the grass nearby.

Earlier that year, in April 1805, the Manchester artist Charles Gough had set out on a cool Lake District morning to walk over Helvellyn. He had no specialist clothing or equipment, only the company of his faithful dog Foxie. Ordinarily, he might have found a guide to steer him safely past the hazards of Striding Edge, but the local militia were out training for the Napoleonic wars. And besides, Gough was known as a 'venturesome spirit', a proud risk-taker. He could go alone. He set off into the morning with a spring in his step. But Gough never arrived in Grasmere. Three months on, the only records of his climb were the clothes and bones the shepherd stumbled across and the remarkable resilience of Foxie. Gough had fallen from a ridge and sustained a fatal wound to the head, but his dog had survived and, remarkably, even given birth to a pup, which hadn't lived long in the harsh conditions on Helvellyn. As a Carlisle newspaper reported later, it seems likely that the dog had eaten the flesh of her master to sustain her. Yet the story seized upon by Romantic poets like William Wordsworth was an alternative one, a tale of heroism and dependability: the faithful hound had loyally stayed by Gough's side, refusing to abandon him. Gough's demise was investigated by Simon Morley in *The Unfortunate Tourist of Helvellyn* and is still commemorated today in an ale from Tirril Brewery called 'Charles Gough's Old Faithful'.

Our cultural preference for this narrative over the more sinister truth says something – I think – about how we see the relationship between dogs, climbers and mountain environments; how we seek out stories of protection, companionship and noble suffering. Tales of faithful hounds are part of our cultural history: a stone's throw from my house in Sheffield, over the border into the Peak District, there's a memorial at Derwent reservoir to Tip, the loyal sheepdog who stayed by his dead master's body through a harsh winter. One icy day in 1953, shepherd Joseph Tagg had gone to tend his sheep in the Upper Derwent Valley. 'Old Joe' was found frozen to death fifteen weeks later. Tip had survived 105 days by his side in one of Derbyshire's chilliest winters. In recognition, she was presented with the canine equivalent of the Victoria Cross, the bronze medal of the Canine Defence League. The memorial above the reservoir was paid for using public funds. Meanwhile, in Wasdale, Cumbria, walkers can visit a new mountain rescue hut which was partially paid for with money raised after a dog went missing on Scafell Pike in 2014. Adam

Nolan's border collie, Jasper, vanished during a walk up the mountain. His #FindJasper campaign on social media went viral and led to Jasper being found by the Wasdale Mountain Rescue Team in a search which lasted four days. In response, Nolan organised a JustGiving page, which raised a total of £63,000. Like the memorial to Tip, the hut is a physical embodiment of the close bond between dogs and people in the hills.

Dogs specialise in getting on with humans. They've been selectively bred for this for the past 50,000 years or more. They can even mimic human actions as well as a toddler can, reacting to our social cues. No wonder we live in a world full of dog lovers, a world where many of us count dogs as members of the family. We're fascinated by them: either anthropomorphising our pets or obsessing about the ways they differ from us. And mountains – theatres of risk, drama and heroism – provide the perfect stage for us to enact our canine fascination in all its pathos and poetry. In short, the hills bring into focus just how much we love being with dogs.

Sometimes, that love makes us burn with collective anger. In August 2012, a dog was abandoned high on Mount Bierstadt in Colorado, USA, a 14,264-foot peak with a notoriously tricky sawtooth ridge. The German shepherd breed – known as Missy – was found by two hikers with her paws cut to ribbons and her saliva blue from dehydration. It took a superhuman effort to get Missy down from the mountain. The first rescue effort failed. A party of eight people eventually climbed to her and carted her down in a pack, battling rain and snow on the way, passing her between them to share the weight. When the story of how Missy had ended up stranded at 13,000 feet finally broke and her owner

Anthony Ortolani came forward, he received death threats. When the details of what had happened began to filter out, they were tragic. Ortolani and a friend had got into difficulty with their dog in severe weather on Mount Bierstadt. After trying to use ropes and a harness to lower her from boulder to boulder, and after a useless attempt to shoulder her weight over rough terrain, Ortolani was faced with an impossible decision. Worried about the worsening weather and the condition of his friend, he knew he had to leave his dog behind to save himself. After an exhausting descent, he phoned 911 and was told that sending a human crew up the mountain to try and rescue a dog would be madness. The following day, his boss sent him out of the state for work and he was unable to return to find Missy himself. After reading about the eventual epic rescue online, Ortolani asked for his dog back. He was met with vitriol. Why hadn't he made more effort to save Missy? Why hadn't he posted on forums to seek help, the way the dog's saviours did? Nobody could understand why he hadn't done more after descending the mountain, why he hadn't been tireless in his efforts to save her. Missy was renamed 'Lucky' in recognition of her ordeal, while her former owner received death threats. She had quickly become the focus of the mountain tragedy, far more than any of the humans involved.

Every day across the globe, dogs are part of mountain adventures and misadventures, involved in our triumphs and failures. Some are climbing with their owners, some are helping to rescue hikers who have gone astray, some are escaping and some are facilitating a human notion of escapism. In Canmore, Alberta, adventurer and photographer Rachael Rodgers takes dogs from local animal shelters out into the mountains to play, and posts lively photos of their outings to her Instagram account. Sometimes she takes them kayaking, sometimes for an extreme hike. Older or weaker dogs might be taken out for a scenic picnic. She's been cross-country skiing with huskies and she's even fitted some of her canine companions with a dog flotation device to make sure they stay safe in the water. 'Every breed of dog is an adventure dog,' she says. 'The trick is matching the type of adventure to the dog's personality.' Their faces beam out at the camera, eyes sparkling. Rachael says her experience has shown her that dogs can find joy anywhere as long as they feel safe. Woods, mountains and creeks are all natural environments where humans and dogs lived not too long ago. There could be something innately nostalgic about how they respond to those places, free from the alien stimuli of life in busy cities and towns. There can be no doubt that the dogs Rachael takes into the hills – armed with snacks like turkey and cheese sandwiches or a peanut butter and jam croissant – adore the exercise, new smells and sensations of mountainous regions. But what's less talked about is what function these mountain adventures serve for us humans too, why we're so compelled to take dogs to extreme places, why we might regard them as our best hiking companions. Rachael admitted it wasn't a question she'd thought about much before:

> 'I love being in the mountains, but my experience is quite empty if I don't have a dog with me. The joy I get from adventures is nearly completely correlated to the joy the dog is showing. It makes me happier to watch them experience it than my experience itself. I am so aware of this that I won't go on adventures without dogs; it seems like such a waste.'

The poet Rainer Maria Rilke felt an affinity with dogs, 'these beings wholly dependent on us whom we have helped lift themselves to gain a soul, but for which there is no heaven'.[1] His reaction captures some of the pathos of our relationship with dogs: one founded on profound empathy but also on difference, the unbridgeable gap between our species. How do dogs help us connect with mountains? Are they guides, rescuers, climbing partners or avatars for our disconnected selves? This is the uncertain, curious, questing place my book starts from.

My own first dog and mountain companion Bell died in 2017 in graceful old age. She had run with me all across the Lake District and Derbyshire, climbed Scottish Munros and curled at the foot of every crag I climbed at. She'd even guarded my rucksack indoors at Ambleside climbing wall, attracting strange looks from the other climbers. This book is an attempt to understand the singular relationship between dogs, mountains and the people who love them, people who turn to them for solace. But it's also an attempt to make sense of a chapter of my own life. It combines intellectual enquiry – interviews, research and data – with memoir, the insistence of my memories, the experience of becoming a dog owner, how mountains and dogs became an inextricable part of who I am. Over the past year, I have met search and rescue dogs, interviewed climbers, and spent time in the hills with St Bernards, spaniels and strays. I have obsessed about why dogs are woman's best friend, man's best friend – and nowhere more so than in some of our most hostile environments. But whatever evidence I've gathered would seem hollow if it weren't set beside a descriptive account of falling in love with a dog, the story of a difficult, rich, transformative year in the Lake District. You'll find that story woven through the essay-chapters that follow, unpredictable as an unleashed whippet, running wherever the scent seemed strongest, wherever the landscape proved hardest to ignore. I approached this book the way I'd approach a long day in the mountains, knowing where I wanted to go, not knowing what I'd find.

# Bell

I have been running for a long time. Unravelling a spool of breath. I've not lived here long enough to know the landscape by name, but I've found a tarn, a frozen rut of track, the place where a stream used to be. All the time, the lean dog runs ahead of me. I can't call her mine, not yet. She is the colour of musical notation. Something about her body makes me think of a harp. Perhaps it's the broad curve of her chest, its half-wing shape. Or the way her legs grasp up the path like quick fingers, fingers plucking at strings. Sometimes I whistle out her name and she comes back to me for a moment. Bell. It is a high, thin sound. A clear thought. We reach the plateau and the way curves back down into Grasmere. Everything is visible for a moment. Everything is open, white and pale grey. And then she is gone.

A whippet is built to run. Not far, but fast. Its heart is large and slow-beating, often arrhythmic at rest, skittish. But that heartbeat settles when the dog can run, sets into the rhythm it knows best. Whippets run with double suspension gallop: all four legs off the ground twice in each stride, once when the legs are totally extended and again when they tuck under the body. And whippets are built to chase. Rabbits, squirrels, hares. Sometimes a deer. They are quick enough to catch, not always strong enough to kill large quarry. When they track their prey, they excel at leaving the world behind.

The winter I moved to Cumbria, my grandfather was dying. Nobody told me because nobody knew yet. I paced around a house too big for me, putting things in place and then putting them somewhere else. Arranging, admiring. The rooms leaked into each other. On the drive up from East Anglia with all my possessions crammed in the boot, my car had broken down fourteen miles away from the city I'd just left. I sat by the roadside, wondering if it meant I should go back. Then my friends Al and Dor came to the rescue in a shiny people-carrier. I arrived in the Lake District as a passenger, opening bottles of beer with the metal of the seatbelt fastener. It took me a week before I noticed the village silence, the way the rain on the roof amplified it. When the first snow came, I phoned a local animal shelter because I wanted to volunteer as a dog walker.

'Do you mind if I ask you a bit about yourself?'

'I'm a writer. Poetry. I work from home.'

'And what else do you do?'

The pause lasted a half-beat. A whippet-heartbeat.

'I climb mountains. And I like to run.'

'On your own?'

'Yes, I live alone.'

'You might suit a sighthound. Lurcher, maybe. Or a whippet.'

All my life, I've been terrified of dogs. The shape of one in the distance was once enough to make me cross the road, or detour for miles out of my way. I remember the gnat-like Yorkshire

9

terriers from the farm by my parents' house that fastened themselves to my dad's ankles. I remember how he picked me up and held me when I screamed. And in some earlier, vaguer thought, I remember another dog, another more violent encounter. Teeth and breath. When I met Bell, I tried not to flinch from her. She jumped at me and I stood my ground. It was only when I walked her on a lead through Ambleside for the first time that I realised she was more nervous than I was. Cowering. Her face was timid and fractious. Her dark eyes reflected my own face, my own fear.

In her award-winning memoir *H is for Hawk*, Helen Macdonald describes the way her solitude merged with the proud isolation of the young goshawk she was training, a bird she'd taken on while she was still grieving for her dead father. As they lived together, their habits began to merge. She ate little, or ate greedily. She slept at strange times. She avoided people. 'The hawk was everything I wanted to be: solitary, self-possessed, free from grief, and numb to the hurts of human life.'[2]

All creatures change your habits. When you walk alone with a whippet, you train your eyes to look for movement. Height becomes crucial. A rustle in the bushes is amplified. You're not content with the invisibility of sound; you want to see everything. From the first time I ever went to Scotland with my dad and looked down from the top of the Easians to Loch Treig, I've been obsessed with high places. I go to the hills to help me think. I run up a mountain when I want to leave my mood at the bottom, balance up tiny gritstone holds when I want to forget. The first time I saw Bell leap up on to a drystone wall on the way down from Easedale and walk along it carefully, I realised height gives you control. A vantage point. She padded along for a stretch, head darting to either side. Then she leapt down gracefully and trotted by my side.

Whippets were originally small greyhounds, deemed unsuitable for hunting because of their size. Over time, they became popular for catching rats and hunting rabbits. They were often taken on by families in mining communities across the north of England who used them for racing and sometimes gave the puppies to their children for warmth – a whippet curled up on the bed at night makes an admirable hot water bottle. There's something almost comical about a domestic whippet: the way they lie on the sofa all day, shiver at draughts and pace the house until they've found the comfiest spot. Their devotion to human company is almost heart-rending. But out in the open, everything changes. The first time I lost Bell in the woods, I scoured the undergrowth for what felt like hours, crashing through wet bracken and whistling for her, pausing to catch a sound from the heart of the trees. She was chasing a young deer, alive to a shape I hadn't even seen. When she came back, panting, she seemed to have a cool disregard for the hunt she'd just been on, pacing at my side without a glance back into the woods.

The part I've always loved most about running is setting out. The route before you. Closing the door to the house. The faint dream of never coming back. Even when you know where you're going, there's always the sense that you could take another path for no good reason, run on and on until your legs give out. Ever since I was a teenager, I've been escaping down canal towpaths and up mountain tracks, setting out without telling anyone where I was going or how long I'd be. Cross-country races, trying to get ahead of the pack. I'd sometimes run with other people, half-disdainful if they couldn't keep up.

When I went to my grandad's funeral in Birmingham, I had to take Bell with me. She looked tiny on the end of her red lead. None of my family knew about her. When we turned up at my step-gran's door, she was vague with grief. She let the dog in, wide-eyed. In the sad days that followed, I often wished I was back in Easedale, my thoughts tracking Bell, metres ahead of me. I wasn't used to company any more, except the half-company of the local pub, the old men who propped up the bar and only spoke to you if it was important. I walked Bell round the new estates, the suburban streets that held no interest for her, the loud cars. But when I fell asleep with Bell curled up on the end of the bed, I allowed myself to think of my grandad. We were at the athletics track in Wyndley, on a day so hot the red surface seemed to store the sun and reflect the heat back. He was almost completely blind and leaned on a white cane. He wore a pale blue short-sleeved shirt. He had a stopwatch in his hand, even though he couldn't read it. I was too skinny in my red county vest and shorts, uncomfortable in my own skin, squinting and pushing my fringe out of my eyes. He didn't know what I looked like, not really. But he was proud of how I trained. He stood in the sunlight and held the watch. He turned his face towards the sky as if he was checking the sun was in the right place. Then he told me to run.

# Partnership

Chris Bonington is adamant: 'First you become a dog lover – not because you're a mountaineer, but because of your basic personality – and then, if you happen to be a climber, inevitably you take them into the hills.' There are two types of people in this world: those who love dogs and those who haven't spent enough time with them yet. I've carried his words north with me, out of the Lake District and up to Scotland, into a higher, wilder landscape. I turn them around in my mouth like a sherbet lemon.

When Ben Arthur, better known as The Cobbler, looms into view through the mist – a strange, rocky trident over Arrochar – I'm distracted. Where the path snakes away towards the mountain, there's a huge rock, a natural vantage point, and, on top of it, the sleek, alert form of a light brown dog. Its shape is unmistakably hound: a pointer perhaps or a Weimaraner. It stands sentry and looks directly at me, tensed. I feel the focus of its stare, feel sharpened in the landscape. Then, a high whistle and the dog is gone. When I catch up with the group ahead of me, I meet Lexy, a Hungarian vizsla puppy who paws at the stash of nuts and raisins in my pocket. Her face is elegantly wrinkled, giving her a look of permanent bemusement. Her owners – a young English couple – apologise for her enthusiasm. 'She just wants to say hello to everyone.'

As I overtake them and bear left to scramble towards Ben Arthur, Lexy bounds after me, criss-crossing the path, pawing at my heels until she's called back with teasing shouts of 'See you later, then!' I feel self-conscious in my role as a kind of Pied Piper. I'm wearing fell-running shoes, a pair of leggings that I slept in last night and a bright yellow jacket, and carrying nothing but a bottle of water, having sloped off to climb a Corbett on a whim this morning, leaving the writing residency I'm meant to be on behind. Each time I pass a walker with trekking poles, I worry that I must seem either dangerously amateurish or like the kind of person who arrogantly advertises their competence in the hills through a calculated display of nonchalance. I'm also three months pregnant, but they can't see that, of course. I place a hand on my belly as I start up steepening ground.

I first learned to love mountains like Lexy, covering the same ground over and over in bursts of manic energy. When my dad brought me to Scotland for the first time, I was a teenage cross-country running enthusiast with a borderline eating disorder. My hair was cropped short and my bones were prominent. Most Wednesdays at home, I'd do a six-mile run and then sneak out to swim for an hour in the local pool. I'd leave the fat on meat untouched, push potatoes to the side of my plate. When we set off up the Easians above the glacial trough of Loch Treig, I was nervy and impatient, ploughing through the heather and charging back down to meet my dad in his steady, upward progress. My dad joked I was like his friend Bob's collie, doing twice the distance. Two older men mistook me for a boy – 'Here, let this lad pass' – and I was first mortified, then proud, taking it as a sign of my apparent strength. When we reached the first summit, I was already beginning to sag under the weight of my rucksack. A dog like Lexy can cover miles more than a human on an average walk

– GPS tracking devices comparing the routes of owners and their pets show that energetic dogs run at least double the distance. And perhaps part of us goes with them, or wishes it could. Part of us never stops moving, going back and forth, learning the intimate smells of the ground.

Whenever I'm walking in Scotland, I can't help but think of lines by my favourite poet, Norman MacCaig, a schoolteacher who lived in Edinburgh and who loved these hills too. MacCaig spent most of his time in Assynt, excavating and evoking the north-west hauntingly in poems like 'Climbing Suilven', but he also wrote about peaks like Schiehallion and – indeed – about non-mountainous landscapes ('landscape and I get on together well / though I'm the talkative one.').[3] To me, he's our great creative theorist of animals and the mind as well. In a lesser-known MacCaig poem, 'On the Pier at Kinlochbervie', the narrator of the piece tries to comprehend everything about a landscape all at once:

> Everything's in the distance,
> as I am. I wish I could flip that distance
> like a cigarette into the water.[4]

We've all experienced that alteration of scale in the mountains, the way things become close and far at once. Camping in East Greenland by the calving face of the imposing Knud Rasmussen glacier in 2016, I was convinced I could hold out my hand and cup the shelving ice, only to be told it was at least two miles away. I too wished I could 'flip' the distance in front of me. The narrator in 'On the Pier … ' says he longs for 'an extreme nearness':

I want boundaries on my mind.
I want to feel the world like a straitjacket.[5]

MacCaig's poems are full of the implicit belief that what we call the 'mind' is everywhere, at the centre of all things, human or otherwise, and that non-human beings and objects can therefore be said to 'think' in some way. In his poetry, MacCaig often gives agency to inanimate objects, or even suggests there's a superior consciousness at work in the minds of animals. People are not intellectually superior in his world. In fact, they're often stumbling around blindly, trying to find the right words for the landscapes that possess them. Animals and mountains know more than we do. MacCaig seems to believe that all things have an intrinsic nature which humans can only attempt to get close to or uncover – that's why his animal poems often express a distrust of metaphor (a heron 'stands ... wrapped in heron',[6] a goat is described in terms of its 'pure goatishness'[7]). MacCaig wants animals to be themselves, free from our intrusive ideas about them, our foolish attempts at mastery.

It would be wrong to use art in clumsy service of a theory, but in MacCaig's work, I often find expressions that remind me of the Extended Mind Hypothesis, the idea that objects within our environments can function as part of the mind too, that things outside of us help us to think. In 1994, the neurologist Antonio Damasio was already arguing that our bodies help us to make decisions as much as our minds do. His famous case study was a railway worker called Phineas Gage who was damaged in an accident when a tamping iron went through his skull. Gage's everyday cognitive function was relatively unimpaired after the accident, but his personality altered dramatically because his long- and short-term decision-making skills had been impaired. Damasio himself did not subscribe to any kind of Extended Mind Hypothesis, only claiming that the mind is connected to the entire body. However, as Neil Levy points out in his book *Neuroethics*:

> ... if we are forced to admit that mind can extend beyond the skull and into the body, there is little – except prejudice – preventing us from extending it still further ... Why not say that our mind can sometimes, in some contexts and for some purposes, encompass environmental resources?[8]

I think we can go even further. If environmental resources can be part of our Extended Minds, then why not our dogs too? When we bring a dog into a mountain environment, we begin to sense and experience it in a new way. Part of us is holding the whistle, calling the dog back, but part of us is running backwards and forwards, nose to the ground – part of our mind is at grass level, gorse level, rabbit level. Do we envy their immersion in scents we can't experience? When we take dogs up hills, we sometimes experience a strange mixture of embarrassment (the need to apologise to other humans for their enthusiasm or wilfulness) and unbridled, enhanced joy.

In his poetic memoir *Under The Rock*, Benjamin Myers describes how his regular walks around Mytholmroyd and all the darkened landmarks of West Yorkshire were transformed by the acquisition of a Patterjack (a Patterdale terrier/Jack Russell cross), how he discovered that 'a dog is an explorer's best friend ...

every rural lurker's alibi, their gateway and guide. A perfect excuse for tramping and trespass.' Myers's dog, Cliff, rapidly becomes part of his outdoor mind:

> Through this dog I too begin to appreciate the small things often lost in the mad scramble of modern life: how to exist in the moment, or enjoy food after a long breathless walk. See the sea, as if for the first time. Stand ankle-deep, sunken in the ancient wood.[9]

When I arrived to interview Chris Bonington, his house was tranquil and self-contained. I knocked too quietly. At the table, his wife Loreto offered me a fresh mint tea. She'd been tending their garden, watering the plants, checking the leaves on each one the way my mum does at home.

Chris had four dogs and always overlapped them to give the older dog a new lease of life. He still pines for dogs and plans to get a new one when he's more settled. Before meeting Chris, I'd been transfixed by a picture of him holding a border terrier, an image shown to me by the climber and author Ed Douglas. In the black and white photo, Chris is almost obscured by the dog. 'It's not my dog!' he exclaimed. The dog belonged to his niece and it was an opportunistic picture taken by someone for a book of famous mountaineers. He described it as a fabulous portrait of the dog rather than him. It was taken after Chris's last dog, Jessie, died. Later, I walked past the wall where the picture was taken, trying to imagine the scene in black and white.

The quartet of Bonington dogs included Bessie, a pedigree Staffordshire bull terrier who was 'gutsy' in the mountains, a law unto herself, a dog who liked to lead the way. After buying Badger Hill in 1971, Chris and his first wife Wendy acquired Bodie (Bodicea), a 'liquorice allsort' of a dog from a litter in Sutherland. Next came her daughter Bella, an exuberant chaser of animals; and then Jessie, a collie/Labrador cross. They also looked after Sensi, a pit bull who had belonged to Chris's son Joe before he moved to Australia. Sensi was so loyal that she had once cornered Joe's landlord when he called round and entered the flat without permission. Sensi never hurt the landlord, but wouldn't let him move from the corner she had backed him into.

Chris still remembers climbing with his son Joe on Gillercombe Buttress on Green Gable and leaving Bodie at the bottom of a route called Grey Knotts Face (HD). Halfway up, they realised Bodie had joined them. Equipped with just two or three slings, Chris was forced to tie one around the dog's waist, the other on to Joe's harness and then do a diagonal scramble to get off the climb. Joe followed with Bodie clipped on to his waist harness, risking a huge pendulum if he had fallen. On another occasion in north-west Scotland, Bodie followed Chris up a technical slab: 'You've got to think of how the dogs will cope with the terrain. I took them on scrambles.'

Chris and Wendy's final dog, Jessie, was brave but not as nimble as Bodie:

> 'The worst thing I ever did with Jessie was to take her up Blencathra on an icy Boxing Day. We got to the crux and she jumped, missed her footing and went down on the right hand side where it goes into a gully. She kept on her feet for quite a long time, glissading down before she finally – thank God – came

to a stop. I rushed down to her and all the damage she had was one torn claw ... My God, I got an earful at home for that.'

Chris's first wife Wendy died in July 2014 after being diagnosed with motor neurone disease two years earlier, but she was a constant presence in our conversation – chiding him gently for not being more careful with the dogs, sharing in their adventures. Often, though, Chris was alone in the hills with them: he described a memorable winter ascent of Ben More Assynt accompanied by a small pack of dogs – Bodie and Bella, Bodie's mother Daisy, and a half-sister of Bodie's. He got to the summit in the pitch dark only to witness a fierce fight which had broken out between them. He separated them and descended by the light of a head torch. The image of his dogs snarling and tumbling in the summit snow with the sky going dark behind them is strange, unsettling and lovely. A pack of animated, scrapping dogs, overheard by nobody.

Chris paused. 'The tragic thing is that they don't live as long as you.' I made a glib comment about dogs not living as long as human climbing companions and Chris corrected me: 'Well, I don't know. I've lost most of my climbing companions.' He carried on:

'A dog gives you total, unquestioning devotion whereas your climbing friends ... there's often an element of competition in it. If you look at long-term climbing partnerships, they almost always come to an end. Certainly with me, with Don Whillans ... that came to an end. It was the same with Whillans and Joe Brown. It's a combination of competition and ego.'

Yet dogs share in adventures as intensely. I've met many dog lovers – in particular, many male dog owners who spend time in the mountains – who hint that they secretly (or perhaps not so secretly) prefer dogs to people. But nobody had expressed it as powerfully as Chris. Towards the end of our conversation, I asked if there was anything else I should be thinking about. Chris became silent for a long time and struggled to speak. He looked as if he was on the crest of a wave of grief, one that had broken and broken over the years and lost none of its force.

'I think after I lost Wendy, going for walks round the block ...
if I'd had a dog, it would have meant a lot. Not having a dog,
it really hits you. It still does.'

When I left the house, the lanes towards Keswick were eerily quiet. I thought about what Chris had said about the death of climbing partnerships and the enduring love of dogs. In the past, I'd often joked to people that my dogs had outlasted any of my relationships. All the journey north to Scotland, I wondered whether the jokes mountaineers tell about their bond with animals and how they surpass any affection for people might cover a more fundamental inability to connect with humans, their complexities, their capacity to disappoint. It's something I've felt myself again and again, crying into a whippet's fur, trusting a dog to comfort me.

As I descend from Ben Arthur and reach the easier track back towards the Succoth car park, I pass Lexy again, gambolling in the rust-coloured stream with one of her owners. They are absorbed in their tasks: the woman washing something in the river and the dog scratching up stones from under the water's surface. Every so often, the woman pauses just to watch Lexy pick her way upstream and I wonder if part of her is rooting underneath the cold water, finding the lost fragments of the day. I pick up pace on the flatter forest track.

It's still early, so I start the car engine and drive a few miles beyond Arrochar to the Rest and Be Thankful Pass, its elevated grandeur muted today by roadworks, dominating the view. I turn off left and down the access track that leads to Ben Donich, another Corbett. I hear the car click as it locks, shutting the heat inside it. The sun has broken through the shawl of cloud and I feel my limbs loosen. The air smells of felled trees and sheep droppings. The approach to the hillside is short, and soon I'm taking small, quick steps up a winding ridge in near-perfect visibility. There are patches of snow clinging to the higher slopes. I can see back to The Cobbler and there are mountains I can't name stretching into the distance. Loch Restil is behind me, flanked by the bulky shape of a Munro. Later, I could look these hills up and write about them as if I know each one by name, but I prefer my ignorance, these moments of naive appreciation.

I've caught myself starting to think of my unborn child the way I might think of a dog or any other unspeaking companion in the hills – imagining the experience of climbing from another, utterly alien perspective. I've not yet seen the baby on a scan and I'm terrified it might not be real at all. All I know is that – if there is a tiny person being carried up this slope inside me – it already has small fingernails and downy, invisible hair. I've pictured each miniature body part, had dreams where they fall out of me one by one, translucent and spidery, dreams where the skin on my stomach blooms with blood like a sea anemone. Though its existence can't be proved, the foetus is already part of my extended mind, my way of experiencing and making sense of the landscape.

There's no one else on Ben Donich today, though the path is crimped with boot marks. When I reach the summit, I place my phone camera on a rock, set a timer and clamber on to the trig point. I balance on one leg and open my arms to the sky. Now that everything I do is freighted with responsibility, it feels briefly precarious to teeter there, exposed, gloriously alone. But there's nobody to judge me.

My hypothetical child has climbed four mountains now – there were two craggy, breathless ascents in the Sierra Nevada with my partner before I knew I was pregnant. I wonder if unborn babies can feel altitude or sense a change in the air. I wonder if any of the brief and complete happiness I feel in mountains is transmitted. When I've descended a few metres from the trig point, I turn and pause; then I hare back up the slope like Bob's dog to get another look at the view. I'm not ready to leave yet.

# Loughrigg

Bell shudders in the back of the silver hire car. She shudders in the pet shop where I buy her a burgundy coat, fasten it around her slim waist with the Velcro tags. She shudders when I cut the engine in Ambleside and sit with my hands steepled on the wheel. To the north, Fairfield is dusted with icing-sugar snow, and the craggy mountains that form the Horseshoe are like a failed cake, slightly sunken. The village is hushed, an underwater feel to it, people walking as if there's something pushing back at them. Some of the hotels and cafes are closed for winter.

Bell lets out a low whine. When I try to attach her lead and coax her out of the car, she stands upright and rooted, her small paws digging into the upholstery. I crouch so that I'm level with her face. Tremulous nose. Bulbous brown eyes, like the beads sewn into the face of the first teddy bear I had, a gift from my step-gran. An impossibly thin muzzle. Her ears are alert – butterfly wings, set proud against her small skull. She is not a wild thing. I must touch her without fear. She is not the collie who pinned me to the ground as a toddler, hot breath and saliva, pushing me into the muck and straw of the farmyard. I must keep my breathing slow, my hands confident.

I know fear is a culture. Fear is a habit. Fear is the lingering taste of blood and no cut on my lip to trace it to. Fear is empty hands at midnight, the locked French windows. The bank balance.

The alleyway. The tightness under my lungs. The unopened letter. It's the icicle in my stomach when a door slams in the night and a girl laughs in the house next door, a slender coolness that soon melts and leaves me quenched. Fear is the sudden lurch I felt on Tryfan as a child when my dad scrambled up metres behind me, the realisation he could fall. It's the imaginary funeral and the deep, aching absence. But when I look at Bell, her trembling, compact body, I know for a moment that fear is also something natural, not something we've given to the world but something it gives back to us. It is sharp instinct, granted knowledge.

Cynophobia – the fear of dogs – is less common than arachnophobia but it affects millions of people. As well as being knocked down by a farm dog as a child, there are other experiences I remember too. I remember the derelict buildings towards Calow Green that we called the Mystery Farm, how barking would echo from the sheds at dusk even though there was never any sign of life there apart from a rabbit skittering across the yard. I remember walking towards Arkwright with my dad, behind the lodge where the ironworks owner used to live, and two Yorkshire terriers darting out from under the hedge, attaching themselves to my dad's ankles. I remember the uneasiness I felt in a landscape that should have been familiar, the cricket pavilion starred with broken glass, the empty bowling club, the way I longed for murder mysteries on the playing fields, unidentifiable bones. An uneasiness which was really a sense of being lost in my own house. I remember the end of the school holidays and the first walk back to Hasland across the fields, making up stories about the stone lions on gateposts and the statuesque horses behind hedges, how I'd play them back to myself in the classroom to drown out the sniggering, the hisses of 'posho' and 'swot', how I pretended I was a presenter in a film of my own life. In our kitchen, we had a picture of our house from the Victorian era, a rough track outside it, the remnants of an inn, two skinny children staring at the camera. I tried to envisage myself in the picture as if it was something I could recognise. In his poem 'A Hill', the American poet Anthony Hecht describes having an unprompted vision of a strange landscape. He sees:

> ... a hill, mole-colored and bare. It was very cold,
> Close to freezing, with a promise of snow.
> The trees were like old ironwork gathered for scrap
> Outside a factory wall. There was no wind,
> And the only sound for a while was the little click
> Of ice as it broke in the mud under my feet.
> I saw a piece of ribbon snagged on a hedge,
> But no other sign of life. And then I heard
> What seemed the crack of a rifle. A hunter, I guessed;
> At least I was not alone. But just after that
> Came the soft and papery crash
> Of a great branch somewhere unseen falling to earth.

I have never been able to shake the subtle, memorable evocation of a hill that is simply 'mole-colored and bare'. The quiet twist at the end of the poem is that the hill is one that the narrator recognises:

All this happened about ten years ago,
And it hasn't troubled me since, but at last, today,
I remembered that hill; it lies just to the left
Of the road north of Poughkeepsie; and as a boy
I stood before it for hours in wintertime.[10]

When I first read Hecht's poem, I was troubled by it. I had the sense that there was a hill that I could remember, a place both utterly familiar and strange.

Eventually, I take Bell in my arms and lift her from the car. We set off towards Loughrigg, the benign, rising hulk of the fell hardened by winter, the bogs made solid with ice. Leaving the houses behind, it's like my first week in Grasmere when the cottage smelled of rotten apples, sharp and soft at the same time, and I got up at dawn and pulled on my fell-running shoes and took no jacket, and ran into Far Easedale until the hills closed over me and I knew I was a wound, healing on the side of the mountain. I ran without a sense of when to turn back. I didn't want to go back to the bare house with my boxed pictures and books, the silence of my new life. Now that I have Bell, I will never be alone there again. She walks a metre behind me on the lead, her tail a switch between her legs. I want to feel tension in the line, her muscles straining. I want to see her twitch at the Herdwick sheep that graze the fellside.

# #NeverLeaveTheDogBehind

The book smells leathery, musty. It is the colour of dried leaves. When I open *Alpine Studies* by W.A.B. Coolidge, a slightly mournful portrait of a hound stares out from the page. It has large ears and glinting eyes, and rests its paws on a high stool as if it had slumped there, exhausted by the effort of standing. The dog is Tschingel and between 1865 and 1876 she completed thirty peaks and thirty-six mountain passes in indomitable style. Tschingel – named for her crossing of the Tschingel Pass from Kandersteg to the Steinberg Alp when she was just six months old – is perhaps the most notable climbing dog of all time. She was thought to be a small bloodhound or large beagle. But this static portrait remains the only image of her. To visualise Tschingel in animated form, we have to turn to Coolidge's prose instead:

> She had strong short legs and a tail that ended in a brush. She was smooth haired, the colour of her coat being reddish brown, inclining more to red ... her body was not handsome, being too thick-set. But she had a very fine head, large and beautiful brown and most expressive eyes ... from the very beginning she liked red wine, and later came to love weak tea, though this always had such an effect on her nerves that after revelling in this drink, she would retire to a corner, sit down and utter

piercing howls – apparently of excessive and overwhelming pleasure, just as when she heard music.[11]

To form images of Tschingel in the mountains, I thumb through the pages of *Alpine Studies*, smiling at the way Coolidge describes her style of ascent, how 'she had a marvellous instinct for avoiding crevasses, smelling the doubtful spots to see if the snow bridges were strong enough to bear her', how 'the black tip of her nose used to get very sunburnt so that the skin peeled off', how she was always roped when crossing glaciers, how her feet were cut by the ice when descending the 12,044-foot Blümlisalphorn in 1868.[12] Perhaps the most striking visual description of Tschingel comes from Coolidge's account of climbing the Aletschorn (13,721 feet) on a day when his aunt had gone up the Sparrhorn to spectate: 'We waved Tschingel in the air as a sort of red flag as the colour of her coat made her a conspicuous object against the white snows.'[13]

Tschingel was gifted to an eighteen-year-old Coolidge by head guide Christian Almer in 1865 to console him after they had failed in an attempt on the Eiger. Had the pair been climbing companions today, I can't help wondering whether Coolidge would have documented his hound's exploits through social media rather than his luminous prose, posting pictures of her at the summit of Monte Rosa, wading through Alpine snow or attempting the rocky descent of Balmhorn. In 2018, celebrity climbers such as Emily Harrington and Cedar Wright fill Instagram feeds with images of their dogs, curled up next to a rope bag or scrambling up vertical slopes. Many amateur climbers and outdoor enthusiasts have followed suit, posting canine pictures taken in extreme or wild environments. Some days, my feed is almost entirely made up of dogs having a good time in the hills.

When free climber, BASE jumper, alpinist and highliner Dean Potter died in a wingsuit flight in 2015, the *New York Post* ran with the headline 'Extreme athlete's heartbreaking final Instagram post' and led with an image of Potter's dog, Whisper, who accompanied him on many of his daring adventures and formed the focus of his short film *When Dogs Fly* (2015). Potter's last post shows a close-up of his dog's snout and whiskers. Whisper, a mini Australian cattle dog, is seen in livid detail: wet nose and sun-dappled fur. The hashtag Potter used to accompany the image is #NeverLeaveTheDogBehind. The same tag appeared elsewhere on Potter's feed, beneath images of Whisper atop Sentinel Dome in Yosemite, Whisper in flying goggles or Whisper peeking from the top of Potter's backpack as he climbs. In one picture, Whisper is seen crouching on a ledge high on El Capitan, staring out at a view we can't see. We feel at once invited into this picture but also excluded, separate from the world which the dog and the man have created between them, unable to go to the special places they can reach. I wonder why a media outlet might consider a final image of Whisper more 'heartbreaking' than a picture of Potter himself. Instagram accounts like Cedar Wright's @allterrainpug attract a following of almost 15,000 people, more than many humans. Looking at them, I can't help thinking there's an aspect of performance in the way we photograph our dogs. The idea that some people might see their dogs as a form of status or a personal statement is relatively uncontroversial (a study of 2,000 dog owners conducted by Frontline Spot On and reported in *The Telegraph* in 2014 claimed a link between dogs and the personalities and even financial status of their owners) but it takes an imaginative leap to conclude that climbers might be using photos of their outdoor-loving dogs to enhance their own image – it seems almost cynical.

I'm tired, my eyes aching and my limbs heavy, the way they always are after a morning at my desk, a day when I've spent too long checking my phone, scrolling through my emails and just waiting for something to happen. There's a fine mist of rain beading the window, but I put *Alpine Studies* down, get on my bike – a mountain bike, too heavy for the Sheffield hills – and leave my suburb behind, panting my way over Brincliffe Edge and up towards Ringinglow Road, the whole world sloping steeply ahead of me. It feels as if the city is trying to shake me off. I'm heading for Hathersage where my friend Jon works in a climbing shop with his liver-and-white springer spaniel, Polly. Polly is lithe, sinewy and obedient. Her face is lit with kindly intelligence. In the shop, she pads around behind the counter, or curls up on the chair where people like to sit to try on rock boots. Children come in just to pat her. Friends call by and offer to take her out walking with them. Tourists sneak her dog treats. Polly is Jon's child, best friend, truest companion. They swim together in the millpond, even in winter. She sleeps at the foot of his bed each night. At the crag, she sticks close to him, loping away but always coming back again.

When I walk into the shop, Polly flies towards me, silken and wild. When Jon slips the lead around her neck, she yanks me through the doors in her excitement to get out, up to Carl Wark or the Plantation. When we pass the last cottage on the lane, I let

Polly go free and she belts towards Stanage, tongue loose and ears slick. I take a photo of her by the gate and send it to Jon on WhatsApp. We always trade pictures of Polly on her adventures, but Jon seldom puts pictures of his photogenic best friend on social media. I wonder what makes him different. There are so many theories about how we project ourselves online. Since Instagram launched in 2010, those wishing to understand its role and impact have looked back to the sociologist Erving Goffman and his dramaturgy of self-presentation (1959): the idea of a performance which seeks to project a desirable image in front of an audience. This contrasts with 'backstage' behaviour in which people might reveal other (by implication less desirable) facets of their personality. An everyday phrase for this might simply be 'putting on a front'. I might apply Goffman's theory to the 'wellness' movement on Instagram – people who promote healthy eating, mindfulness and exercise, the endless images of chia seed porridge, yoga poses and avocado toast I scroll through when I'm bored, imagining the tiny square images as portals to a better life. Some members of that community present stylised and curated versions of their 'backstage' activity too (presumably to make themselves appear more relatable): recovering from a workout or preparing food. If there is a 'mountain community' on Instagram, we might assume it contains some similarity to the 'wellness' movement, but it is also distinct, characterised by the impulse or tendency to document activity and environment. I wonder how much the pictures are staged (did the dog happen to curl up next to the rope bag or was it placed there?) and whether we see our adventurous dogs as extensions of ourselves or as substitutes.

In my favourite photograph of my dog Bell, her slim, whippet shape is foregrounded, dark against a white river of snow and the dawn light, an egg cracked over the Cumbrian mountains. The ground is lit with frost and there's snow on the distant summits. Bell is almost exactly in the centre of the image. She's sitting down – unusual for a whippet – and her neck is craned slightly towards the camera, her ears alert. She's still wearing the slim red collar she had when I first got her from the rescue centre. We'd camped near Sergeant Man on a night much too cold for camping and Bell had shivered at the foot of my sleeping bag all night. I took the picture first thing after taking down and packing away the tent, and Bell was still sitting shivering in the place where it had been. I won't have posted that photograph on social media – Instagram wasn't something I was even aware of in 2010 and my use of Facebook was troubled and sporadic – but the picture was still a kind of performance for me. I wanted to capture dawn over the Lakeland fells, but I wanted to capture Bell witnessing it too. I could have framed the scene without her in it.

I'd not long since invited Bell into my life and the picture was a performance to myself: 'Look, I'm a dog owner now. I see things differently.' Through taking it, I was reassuring myself that I was no longer nervous of dogs after twenty-five years fearing them intensely, that I was a different kind of Mountain Person now. Had I shared the picture on social media, I would have been performing a new aspect of my identity, that of the dog lover, the wild-camper, the woman who subscribed to Potter's maxim #NeverLeaveTheDogBehind. Now that Bell is dead and I've been taking dogs into the hills with me for nearly ten years, the photo performs a different kind of function. In many ways, it is a testament to my stupidity. When I look at the image now, I feel guilty that Bell wasn't wearing a coat on such a freezing morning, knowing how short-haired, skinny dogs can suffer in the mountains. I see my former self – invisible behind the camera lens – as self-centred, thinking about the role of the dog in my outdoors life rather than fully considering the influence I was having on her in the wild places we visited together.

Polly steadfastly ignores the sheep grazing beside the farm. She follows me over a stile, across the road and into woodland. In early summer, these woods are azure, carpeted with bluebells. Polly's legs are decorated with mud, damp and musky. If she strays too far from me, I only have to blow once on the slim orange whistle Jon has given me and she comes back. As I always do when I walk, I'm playing back conversations in my head, poring over things other people have said. A few months ago, I wanted to delve deeper into how mountaineers who post social media pictures of their dogs see what they are doing, whether they think it contributes to a positive self-image, so I decided to invite their responses. Putting out a casual call on Twitter, I was overwhelmed by the interest in my questions – I got written responses by return of email from twenty dog owners (who I'll refer to here by their first names), and photographs from at least half a dozen more. Responses tended to be prefaced with long, personal anecdotes about favourite mountain moments with dogs, recounted with visual clarity and accompanied by photographs. Everyone was keen to tell me about why we like to take so many pictures of our dogs outdoors. Now, my head is full of other people's ideas. Sometimes I have a hard time tuning into the frequency of my own thoughts.

Several people suggested that dogs in mountain environments are inherently less 'self-conscious' in front of a camera. To quote Mickey: 'Dogs don't lie and don't put on a false smile or pose as asked all the time. With a dog, what you see is what you get.' This was echoed by many others. Natalie observed: 'There are a lot of photos of people that are staged; they know their photo is being taken ... and it doesn't capture that moment.' For Neil, this was part of something more fundamental – dogs retain a kind of innocence in mountain environments, manifested as toughness:

> 'They're unaware, or unconcerned by exposure or the elements where a person might be. So it could be a photo of the most grim times, but the dog will probably be coping relatively happily with it because they're with the people, and that's usually all they want really.'

Natalie's response suggested to me that there's a tension between 'being in the moment' in landscape and being self-aware, or even being aware of the photographic process. Do mountain enthusiasts sense a kind of 'authenticity' in the responses their dogs have to mountain environments that they suspect other people lack? How can we be sure that dogs are incapable of artifice and performance? This way of being with dogs in mountains suggests a great deal of inference on the part of the human dog lover. It seems to both anthropomorphise them ('dogs are carefree') and 'other' them at the same time ('dogs respond completely differently – they are without self-consciousness'). Can a dog be both like and unlike us at the same time? When I look at Polly streaking through the grass, possessed by her instinct to find a bird and bring it back to me, to do the work she was bred for, I can't see her as anything but wholly 'other'.

How much of the 'unselfconsciousness' that mountain walkers feel their images of their dogs capture is just projection on their part? To conclude that a dog is unselfconscious would be to assert that it has no sense of self, but how can we know that's really the case? Dogs don't recognise themselves in mirrors and often bark at their own reflections (as mine did once in the shop where Jon works, keeping it up for ten minutes, much to the amusement of the staff). But humans don't overtly smell each other when they meet or determine what objects are based on their scent – should a dog therefore conclude, using their own measures, that humans have no sense of self? There was an implication in many of these responses that photographing beings who lack artifice therefore allows access to something inherently more 'natural'. But when I spoke to my friend Lindsey, a writer and photographer, she reminded me of the important relationship between photographer and subject:

'Photographs of people require a different type of "seeing": it's impossible to avoid seeing the person in the photograph in relation to oneself: the person is perhaps happier, stronger, in a better place, perhaps with better clothing, or more friends. The person becomes a model for ourselves. I'm not suggesting envy is always present, only that I think the comparison is probably always made ... Mountains and hillsides seem in photographs a natural habitat for dogs, even though we've domesticated them. People can never fully reclaim the mountain as our habitat, so photographs of people appearing

to do so generate complicated responses which are less
pleasant than simple ones.'

Perhaps I should have asked Lindsey why simple responses are
inherently less pleasant and whether a dog photograph always
generates an uncomplicated response: my own reaction (a mixture
of fondness and guilt) to seeing the photograph of my dog Bell in
the snow, for instance, seems by no means uncomplicated and
perhaps not entirely different from how I might view a photo of a
person with whom I had a long-standing connection. Perhaps the
inherent comparison between human and animal subjects in
mountain photographs was implicit in the questions I asked.
Another friend, the poet Steve Ely, put the comparison more
bluntly:

'When you photograph a dog on top of a mountain you
commemorate that spirit, their achievement and their
unassuming insouciance. When people have photos taken up
mountains it's, "Yaay, look at us and our mighty achievement."
Meanwhile, the dog's cocking its leg up on the triangulation
pillar or eating some sheep shit.'

Steve has a whippet called Kath, the only sighthound I've met
who joyfully appreciates water. I think of Kath now as I watch
Polly plunging into the millpond after sticks, paddling back
towards me with her head held high, smooth as an otter. When
our dogs come back to us, there's always a kind of relief. As if
we imagined they might run into the hills forever and be lost to
us, as if they remind us of impermanence. Several of the people

I interviewed about their photos recounted how they had started walking with (and therefore photographing) dogs in the hills after the loss of a human family member or at a challenging time in their lives, suggesting that dogs might help 'replace' human loss. In particular, it was interesting to note how some of the respondents focused on the relationship dogs have to time, almost in an aspirational sense. To quote Svenja:

> 'I think there's also something about the pure enjoyment that dogs get from being in the great outdoors, and capturing that feeling of being outside, being in the moment, not worrying about the past or the future, and the freedom to roam.'

Another dog owner, Gry, echoed this when she described the process of photographing her pug as a way of inhabiting a moment more fully: 'Something happens in the photo, and maybe in a way, it also connects me more to the situation, contextually, since he is there with me, and wouldn't be there without me, so to speak.' She argued that this might not be particular to mountain environments but to any situation where she might take a photograph of her dog. Clare, however, focused on the uniqueness of the mountain environment as an arena for interactions between dogs and people, and for photographs of these interactions:

> 'When we're at ground (valley) level, we're all more compelled to fit into certain ways of being, often through others' expect- ations, and I think it's no different for dogs, so to see an animal being free to express itself is a joyous thing. I think there's

perhaps some connection with historic images, particularly paintings, of hunting dogs looking majestic in the hills or collies working hard in the habitat for which they were designed.'

The only person I talked to who mentioned the negative possibilities of taking mountain photos was Svenja. Dogs occupy an interesting position in relation to the self-imposed 'pressure' she recounts:

' ... if I'm totally honest, for a while I was also quite active on Instagram, and there was definitely an appeal to being part of that community of Instagrammers that went on adventures with their dog and took amazing photographs. I think photographs are just such a normal part of our existence these days. And I think dogs are particularly appealing because the way dogs are on mountain adventures is pretty much how we aspire to be on mountain adventures. Your dog isn't waking up at dawn for an Instagram-worthy sunrise shot, or recording their run up the mountain on Strava, or wild camping in the middle of nowhere because it makes for a cool story ... '

As if on cue, Polly darts away from me as I try to take another picture for Jon. She shakes her fur and a storm of water covers my legs. Svenja's answer took me back to the notion of the photograph itself, the urge to capture and catalogue moments in mountains, to 'perform' one's enjoyment. There's a great deal of poignancy in her words, a yearning for a less documented life, or for less of a convention to document activities. There's also an interesting paradox in Svenja's argument. Perhaps one of the things that appeals to us about seeing dogs in mountains (and therefore invites us to take pictures of them there) is their apparent unself-consciousness and ability to dwell in the present moment. But maybe the urge to capture that in a photo feeds into the sense of requiring something 'Insta-worthy'.

The conversations I had with people who responded to my questions about their photos seem to support work done by the geographers Thomas Fletcher and Louise Platt, who argue that:

> It is no longer sufficient to simply incorporate, represent and ultimately define animals as 'other' presences and bearers of meaning within humans' cultural spacings and placings … Instead, animals should become, in Whatmore's (2006) phrase, 'agent provocateurs' for thinking about ourselves … [14]

Based on face-to-face semi-structured interviews with twelve respondents, Fletcher and Platt looked at the ways in which dog walkers constructed their walks and reflected on the process of walking with an animal. Like my respondents, their interviewees were influenced by notions of their dogs having distinct personalities and manifesting some of their 'dog-ness' in open spaces, something that might be suppressed in domestic settings: the notion that dogs are 'free' and 'more themselves' when out on a walk (even if the route has been in part planned and constructed by a human). Similarly, a photo might appear to show a free and guileless dog in its element, yet the 'wildness' of the picture might have been carefully curated by the human companion. Yet perhaps this is nothing new – when Coolidge described Tschingel in his elegant prose, perhaps he really was doing the equivalent of staging a mountain photograph of his beloved companion, creating an image which would reflect well on him as her human guide as well as giving life to her as his faithful and intrepid pet.

As Fletcher and Platt note, dog walking is an activity which hasn't been studied much outside the field of health and well-being and this is doubly true for the performative act of photographing a dog walk, or photographing a dog in a mountainous environment. Yet these relationships seem to have the utmost significance to humans:

> ... it was while out on the walk that many respondents felt their relationship with their animal was most strongly enacted ... Whilst in many ways the walk may reflect the historical social order of human domination and animal submission ... rather than there being a one-way flow of power, the walk is where humans and dogs *negotiate* power within their relationship.[15]

If the walk is a negotiated activity between species, a place where humans give up some of their power, then a photograph of the dog returns control over the performance of that walk to the human. As the responses I gathered from mountaineering dog-lovers suggested, many people who take their dogs into the mountains claim to do so because they enjoy seeing them experience those environments in a way that seems less self-conscious and less time-bound than humans. But witnessing that apparent freedom in an animal can still produce the urge to represent it, to take an image that will last beyond the moment, to create a means of performing the triangulation between dog, human and hillside to other people and – implicitly – to get their approval. The moment passes.

The photograph is shared. The dog walker checks their phone for 'likes'. The dog continues to run through the bracken, on towards the next hill.

Whenever I let Polly off the lead to hare after ripples in the grass or allow her to nose around the heather, there's a definite negotiation of power going on, the kind Fletcher and Platt talk about: sometimes I want to turn back, but it's clear that Polly wants to sniff at one more wall, or dive in one more bog. The look she gives when her lead emerges from a pocket is heartbreaking. *Go on*, I think as I pocket the lead again, *be a dog*. Then I smile to myself and walk on, following where she takes me. We have all the time in the world. And today, I don't need my phone camera to prove it.

# Grasmere

It rains and she will not stop barking. Shrill, harsh and insistent. Her voice cuts through silence the way her body cuts through a field. The rain paws at the dark window. It throws its body against the door. Bell barks when I shut the door to the bathroom. When I try to walk to the shop, she howls and pisses on the floor. When I try to close the kitchen door as she eats her breakfast and I sit down to write, she tears at the lino with her teeth. Once, she gnaws at her own leg.

It is winter and I have invited a black dog into my home. In British folklore, the black dog is a hellhound, a nocturnal apparition, a shape-shifter, a portent of death. There's a story at the front of David Bell's volume of collected *Derbyshire Ghosts & Legends* flippantly titled 'Beware of the Dog!' Every time I see the book on my shelf, I feel compelled to read it. I've been doing this for so long now I almost have the words by heart. The tale is set in Bradwell in the late 1700s and concerns two brothers, Will and Sam, who both worked in the local mines. Returning home late one night after playing cards, Sam was stopped dead in his tracks by the chilling sight of a giant black dog. He pointed, shaking, while his brother could only implore, 'What yer staring at?':

> Sam could not believe that his brother was unable to see what was plainly in front of them ... it was so near that he

43

could feel its hot breath on his face but as he stood in
petrified silence the dog vanished before his very eyes.
When he recovered his voice, he explained what he'd seen
but his brother would have none of it. 'Naw, Sam,' he laughed,
'there wiz nowt there.' The two argued for the rest of their
journey home ... [16]

Next day, Sam tried to convince his brother that neither of them
should go to work down the mines. But while he stayed at home,
Will dismissed his superstition and set off for their shift as usual.
Later that day, a roof collapsed in the mines and Will was killed
beneath the weight. The black dog that Sam saw had been a
warning, fatal to ignore. There are other apparitions in Bell's book
of stories – mermaids, grey figures, horses and haunted children
– but none as chilling as that omen of collapse, of terror under-
ground, of miners stifled by falling rubble. It also evokes the
ordinary, melancholy north-east Derbyshire of my childhood,
the silent pits and mineshafts, the village at Arkwright that moved
across the road because of open casting, the trees felled in
the field.

The connection between dogs and death might stem from
Cerberus and his role as the guardian of the underworld, from the
image of dog as scavenger. I once wrote flippantly about Cerberus
in a poem, a piece about my grim surname, its translation as 'death'
in French and the reluctance of a French boating crew to let my
family sail: I imagined 'a thick Alsatian with a face like Cerberus
ushering us into port'. The poem was as much about my fear of
myself as any omen, my fear of becoming:

... the girl
who takes the worst route home, pauses

at the mouths of alleyways, or kisses
strangers on the nameless pier; eyes open,
staring out to sea, as if, in the distance
there's the spindle of a shipwreck,
prow angled to a far country.

In the draft of that poem ('The French for Death') that made it into my first collection, I cut the image of Cerberus from the early stanzas, finding the dig at once too comical and too grotesque.[17]

Most mornings, it's too half-lit and too wet to get up and go outside. I try to pull the duvet over my head and Bell doesn't stop me, only whining when she needs to go into the garden to pee. Ever since Winston Churchill popularised the phrase 'Black Dog' to describe the bouts of depression he experienced throughout his life, dogs like Bell have also been a metaphor for mental illness. Even when the sun drags itself over Helm Crag and the hills to the north, Bell shares my apathy. The first walks I take her on round the village are cursory. I move quickly, nodding to people I recognise, hoping that nobody stops to say hello. We become shadows. When it goes dark – early and without warning, the stars above the hills extinguished – I put Bell's lead on and we go to Tweedies bar where I order pints of sharp, sweet cider. I always have one more than I should. There are tourists poring over maps they haven't been able to use, ordering small portions of fish and chips. There are solitary men whiling away the hours after a shift at the bar, men who build drystone walls and work in climbing walls. There are nervous interns from The Wordsworth Trust cradling lime and soda, sharing a bag of salt and vinegar, trying to make their living allowance last the week. The fire has been lit. When Bell begins to bark under the table, I have to leave.

# The faces of saints

Syrah lifts her huge, jowly face towards me. I ruffle her fur, pressing down on her strong skull. We've been told not to stroke the dogs too much, not to irritate them by fussing their ears and solemn heads. They are not pets. As we take the stony track that climbs east from the Great St Bernard Pass, Syrah's gait is measured, each step exact. There's something of the lion in the way she walks, loping and prowling, surprisingly easy to handle on her thick lead. Behind us, summer storm clouds are moving in from the Alps and the other dogs are restless in their kennel. Syrah moves slowly up the steepening gradient, only quickening when we reach a flat patch of grass where she sniffs excitedly. 'Marmots,' our guide announces. 'When she finds one, it doesn't last long.' We climb higher towards a pewter-coloured lake and the rough-cast shapes of mountains. I have almost forgotten the pass, the church in the hospice with its black Madonna and abundant, decaying sunflowers, the museum with its stuffed, life-size dog – a tribute to a St Bernard who slipped into a ravine in 1910, guiding a friar towards a traveller.

We came by efficient train and slick bus from the Swiss town of Martigny, climbing through a series of small settlements, each seeming less prosperous than the last. The Great St Bernard Pass was once the major route for travellers to reach Italy, across to Aosta, but the hairpin bends and lofty drops have been superseded by other routes. Yet, arriving at the top of the pass, there's still the sense of a frontier – I could almost imagine Napoleon settling his troops, turning the hospice into a barracks, building a base from which to stage his assault on Southern Europe. Innocuous in summer, the pass must be a different proposition in snow. It was here in AD 926 that Augustan monk St Bernard de Menthon founded a hospice and monastery to shelter travellers on the treacherous route through the Alps, and it was here that the monks began to breed these loyal, loping mastiff dogs which bore his name.

St Bernards are giants. If Syrah put her paws on my shoulders, she could easily floor me. I think of the puppy in saccharine American film *Beethoven* who quickly grows into an adult capable of wrecking each room in the house. In one scene, Beethoven's eager new family are shown carrying enormous sacks of dog food. The average weight of the breed is between 65 and 120 kilograms – though some weigh more – and the approximate height at the withers is seventy to ninety centimetres. 'Withers' is a word which always makes me think of diminution, of shivering, almost, and it's strange to hear it in relation to gentle giants like Syrah. Their coats can be either smooth or rough. They are jowly and wrinkled. There's something autumnal about the way they look, their fur colour typically a red shade with white, or a mahogany brindle, the shade of conkers. Their faces and ears are often tipped black. Syrah is the colour of my Grandma Mort's hair and a desk Grandad Mort used to own in Oldham, overly polished. Their fur looks weighty, lustrous. Even their tails are heavy and low-hanging. When you look into a St Bernard's face, you get the sense that everything is being pulled earthward – it can give their eyes a bloodshot appearance.

The earliest written records of the dogs here at the pass are from 1707, though some paintings depict them earlier. Back down in Martigny at the museum dedicated to the dogs, a series of images show St Bernards dragging travellers from the snow while blizzards rage around them, carrying children on their backs. Their faces are always drawn in an unusually expressive way, as if the dogs seem animated by the anguish of their task. In the town, we're staying on the Rue des Marroniers. 'Marron' brings to mind the chestnut colour of the dogs. Marroniers were mountain people who acted as early guides to pilgrims and merchants, forming rescue teams in case of danger. In 1129 Rodolphe, abbot of St Trond in Belgium, described them in high boots with iron nails, holding long sticks to help them feel a path through the snow. They were often accompanied by the dogs. The image of St Bernards as rescuers is enduring. In fact, they were originally intended to protect the monks from bands of brigands who roamed the area, preying on pilgrims in the pass. Rodolphe described the tribulations facing those who wished to cross the Alps in his account of a caravan leaving Saint-Rhemy:

> It was high morning and the pilgrims, full of fear and trembling, were preparing themselves to face menacing death by holy prayers. They were fighting each other to be the first to be confessed by the only priest, and as he was fully occupied they were confessing to each other their sins. As they were busy accomplishing this duty in the church, terrible news arrived: ten of the guides who had left the village earlier had been swallowed by an enormous mass of snow and carried away into the abysses ... [18]

A morgue was built in the pass in 1476 and kept the remains of some two hundred cadavers, mostly mummified by the cold.

St Bernards became renowned for being able to sense impending avalanches as well as for their utility as rescue dogs and excellent sense of direction in snow and fog (aided presumably by a keen ability to scent). By the mid eighteenth century the breed was regularly accompanying monastery guides through the St Bernard Pass, leading guides and mountain travellers to the safety of the hospice. It is thought the Saint Bernards kept at the hospice were responsible for locating no less than 2,000 lost, stranded and avalanche-trapped travellers during the three centuries for which the hospice has kept records. During the harsh winters of 1816–1818 in Switzerland, there were increased numbers of avalanches and as a consequence, many of the dogs themselves were killed. Around 1830, this is said to have led to a brief period of importing Newfoundland dogs from the Colony of Newfoundland, which were crossed with the short-haired St Bernards, and so the long-haired or 'rough coat' St Bernard was born. This was a short-lived experiment: the longer-coated offspring were prone to catching snow in their curls where it would harden in the cold and form into ice. The cross-bred puppies were either sold, given away to farmers in the lower villages or exported out of Switzerland.

In a museum devoted to the dogs, we wander idly through the gift shop. There are stuffed St Bernards of every shape and size, some glove puppets, some enormous, realistic models. My partner Jess holds one up and stares at its glassy face. We are looking for the perfect gift for our child-to-be, a toy that will be his guardian. On holiday in Greece earlier in the summer, I cried with joy at the sight of a small boy with a soft toy beagle which he took everywhere with him, perched it on the edge of the breakfast table while the solicitous waiters pretended to serve it food. I clutched Jess's arm and wept. I want our baby to have a toy like that. What I really want is for something to guard him in the womb, bring him into the world unscathed. I don't think I am enough for him. I'm afraid that I've already done things wrong. By one of the display cabinets Jess is gesturing excitedly.

'Look! This is perfect!'

He's holding a large, slim book with a moonlit, snowy cover, a child in a red bobble hat clinging to the back of a giant, benign dog who lifts his nose up to sniff the air. We open the pages and start to read together:

> It was on a cold, dark night that three small St Bernard puppies came into the world, in a solitary monastery high up in the Alps. One of them was Barry. The puppies' mother lay in freshly laid straw and lovingly licked her newborn young. Next to her knelt the young monk Benno. He stroked her fur gently. 'What beautiful, healthy puppies,' he said softly. 'This one here is the last to be born. But he is the biggest and the strongest. He looks almost like a little bear, with his large head and his broad muzzle.' Benno cradled the little puppy in his arm. 'I will call you Barry, little bear. That name suits you well.' The little puppy raised its head, as if he had already recognised his name and snuggled up to his new friend.[19]

The name Barry comes directly from 'bari', which means 'little bear' in the dialect of Berne. For me, 'Barry' had always reminded me of one half of the comedy TV duo The Chuckle Brothers, their slapstick, ineptitude and wordplay. Two brothers from Rotherham, Barry and Paul. The bear-like origins of 'bari' sound rather noble. The children's book we are rapt by is based on the life of a notable St Bernard from the monastery who really was given that name. Barry lived from 1800 to 1814 and rescued more than forty people from the mountains around the St Bernard Pass. He served humans in the harsh conditions of the pass for twelve years before being retired in Berne, far from his original mountain home. Because of his reputed courage and supernatural sense of danger, Barry has become a legend and his body was kept for posterity after his death, embalmed in the Natural History Museum in Berne. It is settled. We buy the book and a stuffed dog with a thimble-sized barrel around its neck. Our son can be watched over by Barry the stuffed St Bernard, and as soon as he's old enough, he can read Barry's story too. We leave the museum and realise we are hungry. We begin scanning the cafes for somewhere we can eat fondue, huge gloopy trails of cheese you have to wind around your fork.

The iconic barrel so often shown in pictures of St Bernards, hanging from the dogs' necks and reputed to contain brandy, is, of course, likely to be a myth. As the story goes, the stuffed version of famous Barry languished for a while in the museum basement where workers would go to eat their lunch. One museum worker left his portable wine barrel hanging from Barry's neck and the curators decided to leave it there when his image was resurrected. I once saw a St Bernard resting in Grindelwald with a huge barrel hanging from it. The dog looked perplexed, weighed down by its cargo.

It has begun to rain. Huge droplets, the size of paws. If it can rain cats and dogs, I wonder what it would be like if it rained St Bernards. When we returned Syrah to her kennel, her fur had begun to release a keen, musky scent. The other dogs were barely attentive when she came back, lifting their jowly heads briefly from the floor and then going back to their repose. I think of the huskies I saw in Kulusuk, Greenland in 2016, and how these huge mountain dogs contrast with them. I'd gone to East Greenland to camp by the calving face at the end of a fjord for several weeks and explore the peaks beyond the Knud Rasmussen glacier. Kulusuk is a small settlement of 250 people, battered mercilessly by the elements, and when I approached on foot from the miniature airport, the first thing I noticed was the town tip, rusted agricultural equipment, tyres and rubble strewn beside the colourful houses. Boys were playing football down by the harbour. Then I noticed the dogs, wolf-like and alert, all chained up at intervals apart from one another. My guide warned me never to walk too close to them lest they attack. That night, I lay on my bunk bed and listened to their howls as they ricocheted across the night. One would start it off with a mournful bay and then it would be picked up by the others, tossed backwards and forwards in the air. It was impossible to sleep.

Huskies are a sled-type of dog bred in northern regions to pull loads fast. They are related to the Alaskan malamute, a larger, older breed of dog used to carry heavier loads at a slower pace. My friends in Chesterfield own a malamute, a stately, bulky dog called Gerrard who moults on the carpet and who – as a puppy – liked to play by gently biting my arm and tugging at it. I can't shake the idea that huskies and malamutes, with their piercing eyes and power to break free and run, aren't really pets. There's something of the wolf about them. The word 'husky' comes from a word used to refer to Arctic people – the word 'Eskimos' pronounced 'Huskimos' by English sailors on trading vessels. The kinds of huskies found in Greenland share an ancestry with the Taimyr wolf of North Asia, a breed now extinct. There is also a specific breed of husky-type called the Greenland dog, specialised in hunting polar bears and seals.

Dogs first appeared in Greenland around 4,000 years ago. The huskies who kept me awake at night in Kulusuk seemed to sing their ancientness, proud above the sturdy roofs of the houses. As I packed my things before dawn, nervously checking and rechecking my rucksack, I felt like an interloper in the vastness of ice. I thought of them often when I was out on the fjord, crossing huge glaciers with their bottomless, blue crevasses. All night at camp, it was the crash of calving ice that kept sleep locked away from me, not the bay of the dogs. When we rose early and put on crampons, struck out towards the mountains, I thought of their steadfastness. One day, we spent eight hours crossing the crevasses, roped together, judging each step and leap. When the day was over, I took off my rucksack and cried. I was overwhelmed by a sense of my own smallness, how insignificant we all were in this library of ice. I was taken over by the impostor syndrome I've sensed my whole life, only this time it was warranted: we were all impostors against the flanks of cold, the shifting, restless glaciers whose movement we had helped to generate. We were guilty, we were cause and effect. As Seamus Heaney might have said, we found ourselves lost yet at home in this most un-human, human-shaped environment.[20]

Writing in the *Huffington Post* in 2017, Mike Arkus tried to describe an outing with sled dogs in Greenland:

> You don't try and pet the Greenland sled dog with a cheery Mickey Mouse-like 'Come here Pluto', a pat on the head and a treat in your hand, because the treat will be your hand ... So you stand back and admire them from a distance as they howl and yelp and rear up and charge around their myriad enclosures, as they are now doing on the outskirts of Ilulissat here on the west coast. In fast there are almost as many dogs here as the 4,500 inhabitants.[21]

Returning to Kulusuk after weeks of isolation on the glacier, our conversations mostly about altitude and the movement of ice, I felt dizzy and drunk as I stepped off the boat. We'd been speeding for hours back towards the eastern settlement, whales in the water behind us, a clutch of white gulls who turned as one so that they were suddenly black. Walking through the town, I strayed slightly from the path and a husky lunged at me, a snarl of yellow teeth and white fur. On our last day, we packed our climbing shoes and went bouldering at a small crag behind the furthest houses. Three husky puppies followed us, skittering along the path and yipping excitedly. As I climbed, one of them delved into my rucksack and retrieved a sock. I chased him through the grasses for hours as he gambolled and rolled, smelled the musk of his fur close up.

St Bernards may look calm and placid but – despite their history of aiding climbers – they are not tame dogs. At the St Bernard Pass, children are warned not to stray too close to the pens, feeding is strictly forbidden and pet dogs (or 'personal dogs' as the guidelines amusingly call them) are not allowed on the walks for fear of them being attacked. W.A.B. Coolidge's mountain dog Tschingel was often attacked by St Bernards in the stopping-places they found in the mountains, mauled viciously by some. Nowadays, St Bernards are mostly bred for the museum or exported to other countries as pets (though they may be temperamentally unsuited for many of the climates people want to keep them in). A few are still trained to work as avalanche dogs. But mostly, they have been supplanted by smaller, lighter, lither breeds like the German shepherd who can also help dig people out of snow burials but who have the advantage of being easily transported in helicopters. St Bernards live on as an emblem of the mountains and of our companionship with dogs in the harshest environments, but they are no longer working dogs.

I can't help feeling a stillness and sadness around the former monastery in the pass. Jess has read about a Salvator Rosa painting which depicts one of the St Bernards and is still kept in the hospice building. We google it – regal lines and warm colours, a departure from Rosa's other work. It is cast in the yellow hues of something strange and ancient. When we show the image eagerly to staff in the hospice and ask them where we can see it, nobody knows where it can be found. Some of the museum workers believe it is there, you just have to ask the right person. Others shrug, or look at us with suspicion. We start to doubt our judgement. A man directs us to a room where there are religious paintings, relics but no dog. We walk gingerly up to the doors of private rooms but daren't try them. The hospice is emptying now; perhaps there are secret chambers to open, corridors to linger in. Instead, we step back into summer. We run for the bus in the rain and set off down into the valley with the dogs watching us through half-open eyes.

# Charlie

When I bring the second whippet home, it is a high, clear day in April and Kirby Lonsdale is streaked with sunlight, heat pushing its long fingers through the trees, touching the ground and warming it. The new dog is called Charlie. He has caramel-coloured fur, he's silken and muscular, taller than Bell. His nose quivers with spring. In the fields, he tears apart from us, all haunches and breath, emerging moments later with a rabbit, limp between his jaws. His owner shrugs. 'Plenty round here. He's always catching them.'

Charlie pads over to Bell and carefully places the rabbit at her feet. It is still warm. I almost imagine I can see its sides beating. Working dogs should bring back their catch alive and leave it to their master to dispatch. Charlie is no worker. The rabbit's neck has been efficiently broken. Its ear reminds me of the mermaid's purses I used to collect on the beach as a kid. Bell looks down at the rabbit but she does not even sniff it. She is still, not trembling for once. The two dogs face each other, Charlie's sides still shaking from the effort of the sprint, his tail held high. Then Bell turns and picks her way carefully back towards the house and we follow her. The rabbit is left discarded in the field for the flies and maggots, a bag of fur and blood.

It is almost quarter past three and the man seems anxious on the patio of his smart house. There are roses climbing a trellis outside and the kitchen is pale and metallic, full of gadgets.

'So …?'

'Oh yes, I—'

'They seem to get on.'

Bell is cringing behind my legs, keeping away from Charlie. I can't work out why the man is in such a hurry. Then I look at the clock again. Of course. The kids are due home from school soon. They don't know their dog is being given away. The realisation is a pang in my stomach. I crouch down on the floor and smell Charlie's Hobnob-biscuit fur, ruffle his fur under his ribs. He has a small white bib at the front, similar to Bell's. Then I stand up and lead him to the car. As we pull away and the house becomes smaller in my rear-view mirror, Charlie stands up in his basket, staring back at the fields and the French windows. Then, abruptly, he circles in the basket a few times, flops down and goes to sleep for the rest of the journey.

Back in my cold house – the walls feel like a cold store even at this time of year – I let them sniff around one another. They have a bed each and I've set out special feeding bowls. I give them each a treat: comical, bone-shaped snacks picked up from Booths in Windermere. I sit down and try to start work on the commissioned poem I'm finishing for an event in Manchester. But before long, there's a commotion, growling and a shrill yip. I turn to see Charlie trying to mount Bell, his front paws looped over her. When she snaps at him, he stops. I turn back to my work. This happens again and again as evening settles. There are snarls, anguished howls and a pleading whine from Charlie. He trails Bell round the house. He tries to mate with her, again and again, with stubborn animal persistence. That's the word I think of:

animal. I have to remind myself that's exactly what he is. Once, Bell attacks him and his nose blooms with a vivid red streak. He looks at me almost reproachfully, his eyes imploring. A moment later, he tries to mount her again.

In her book *Afterglow*, Eileen Myles describes the strange and traumatic experience of trying to mate her beloved dog – an adopted pit bull called Rosie – with another dog, Buster. The process becomes tortuous. The humans have to intervene. Rosie tries to fight Buster. They have to muzzle her, raise her vulva towards the male dog. Buster's owner Doug warns Myles that pit bulls 'can be very violent maters'. It is pouring with rain outside. Eventually, things start to progress:

> They simmered. He poked. Slightly. She wavered. Her whole body wavered. The two swaying slightly together. His leg cast over her back. She ceased to turn, their two mouths, their huge jaws slack, hanging open, panting in unison like big smiles wavering in the night. We all sat down and relaxed – though still holding on. I took off Rosie's muzzle but held on to her collar. I felt like she needed me. I had a new experience of my dog's body. She had one. She was being fucked right in front of me. I felt shame. Regret. Fear. Excitement.[22]

Throughout Myles's book, Rosie narrates part of the story, commenting on the humans and their lack of understanding, their failure to grasp the superiority of dogs. It is an enchanting, unsettling read, but this chapter – the one she calls 'The Rape of Rosie' – is perhaps the most unnerving. Afterwards, Myles and Doug go for a walk through streets that shimmer with blackness.

Rosie is bleeding. The dogs need to drink a lot of water. They go to a shop and Myles feels as if she is in someone else's life.

My house is lonely at night. I meet a man on the last bus and talk to him for hours, even though I'm not sure I can trust him. Then there's the barman who only wants to come back after parties. I start up my long-distance relationship again and stop it and start it and stop it again. There are late-night phone calls where I sob down the line about how much I miss my dead grandad and my boyfriend says nothing. I bring someone else home and, in the morning, I want to put on my clothes and slip out until I realise it's my house. The dogs always try to clamber on to the bed; they circle and pant and make sounds of distress. I have long-distance arguments. I lock my door. I buy bottles of red wine and curl up at night with books that make me anxious. *Trainspotting*. All the novels of Graham Greene.

I'm experimenting with leaving the two dogs in the house together while I run small errands, trips to the shop or to the GP surgery. On my way back from the village, I meet Mark, long-serving guide at Dove Cottage, cutting the grass outside the house.

'Your dogs are making a right din. I thought they must be attacking each other.'

'Sorry,' I sigh. 'I thought Charlie might calm Bell down.'

Mark laughs and leans on his lawnmower. 'I love it,' he says. 'You got another dog to calm the first one down and instead, she's just set him off and turned him bad.'

I walk back to my house and unlock the door. I can't argue with him.

# Body

I have never known 'body' as a verb before. I lie still in the long grass and try to become an action, try to become a silence, as archetypal as the Wharncliffe stones. I am a body. I am a pregnant body, only three months away from giving birth, my stomach swollen in a full moon. My body is a part of me. But I am also 'bodying', practising metamorphosis, playing dead while becoming increasingly aware of my breathing, my rising and falling chest, the blood that beats steadily in the vein at my neck. It's almost like meditation, only there's a raw urgency to it.

Months earlier, I stood in a windswept car park at the top of the Kirkstone Pass in Cumbria and watched other people hiding on the fell, crawling behind rocks, burying themselves in the ground. Rob Grange from the Lake District Search and Rescue Dog Association explained the art of 'bodying' to me:

> 'We call them bodies – dogsbodies. If you try to look now you won't see them, but amongst the boulders there are so many places people can hide. If someone is hypothermic, they're going to try and hide. But the dogs will still pick up the scent normally from at least a few hundred metres away. Part of our skill as handlers is working out how the dogs will respond in different conditions and adapting. On scree, the airflow might not be as smooth. It's the understanding between the two

of you, the emotional relationship which is key. You're working your dog, you're watching their body language and they're doing the same thing with you. If I'm not happy, my dog isn't happy. It's like a parent and a child, a husband and wife, that sort of closeness, whatever goes on on the fell.'

Rob has been part of SARDA for a long time, but part of Mountain Rescue for longer. 'We're all members of mountain rescue teams anyway,' he told me. 'We have to be for at least two years before we start. We're at a stage where we can administer drugs on the scene. We use dogs for searching in conditions that are difficult to search in. When it comes down to it, drones and helicopters don't work in really bad conditions and that's when people are really in trouble. We were out the other week in sixty- to seventy-mile-per-hour winds. Dogs with their skills are so much better – replacing a team of eight to ten people with one person and a dog.'

In this age of advanced gear and technology, it seems strange – comforting, even – to think that a dog could be the most efficient means of finding someone, like the loyal St Bernards of the hospice on the Swiss–Italian border, setting out in avalanche conditions with only their keen sense of smell, their strength and their intuition. In Cumbria, I heard high whistles in the background. The car park was beginning to get full, tourists crowding to pet the dogs and find out more about their role. Children wanted to meet them and fuss them, play with their toys. I could make out figures moving on the hillside, Chris and his Labrador Beck. The dog and handler relationship is key, Rob told me. It's not about a specific dog not being suitable; it's about the partnership with a human:

'You could train virtually any dog, but there are dogs more suited to the terrain. Technically, you could get a chihuahua to do it, but ... You need awareness of the conditions you'll be working in. I've got a young border collie pup at the moment. In Norway they're using Malinois, very fast and powerful dogs, very good at digging in avalanches. If you're working in hot conditions, you need a dog appropriate to that, you'd choose a breed more suited to disaster work.'

Bracken arrived then, a border collie, nine years old with a teddy-bear face. Bracken is a graded dog, which means he is fully qualified. Some of the dogs had 'Rescue' written on the side of their bibs to distinguish them. The others wore plain bibs. It takes between two and four years to get graded, at least one night a week, a training weekend each month, and a week a year training on top of the handlers' commitments to mountain rescue. The dogs operate as a service for all mountain rescue teams in the area across the north of Britain. To pass as a graded dog, the teams must prove reliability and consistency in finding bodies. Assessment areas are set up which a team could be expected to cover in around two hours. A minimum of fourteen assessments are required, one of four hours, in all weathers. Footpath searches are required, covering fifty metres to the side of the path, and forest searches, which are navigational exercises. Only then can a dog and handler 'grade'.

'When we're teaching them, we're looking for their motivation,' said Rob. 'It's got to be a game for them. Bracken there likes squeaky toys so he thinks everyone he finds will have one of those on them. Labradors are motivated by food instead! My youngest at the moment loves a particular kind of squeaky ball. When the dog finds someone, they bark to indicate the body. If you can hear them, you follow the bark. If it's out of range, the dog will come back and lead them there.'

On the fellside, Beck stopped. We waited for him to bark to show that he had identified a body, but then he darted off in a different direction. I wandered away to meet Andy Peacock, a handler with an extremely noisy dog. Andy sighed.

'This is my trainee dog, just starting the process. My last was a successful border collie – she had a find in an avalanche in Scotland. This one is called Cirque, the last was called Corrie, so the naming has been a bit sentimental. She is just seven months old. She's a Belgian Malinois – her parents are Norwegian. Border collies are suited for round here. These dogs are extremely agile so I thought I'd challenge myself with one of them.'

Cirque was at pre-stage 1, obedience training. She strained excitedly on the lead and barked vigorously. She had a white bandage on her leg, where she'd caught it on a fence. The Association vet deals with problems like this. To my untrained eye, she looked a little like a German shepherd. But there was something more gaunt about her, more taut, somehow elongated and sharp. Could a whippet ever do this? I thought of their agility, speed and persistence in the chase. Then I thought of their shivering reticence and their short hair. I met an eleven-year-old graded border collie called Einich, part of Coniston Mountain Rescue. Einich is her handler Joy Grindrod's second dog:

'I got her to do the job, though she came a bit sooner than I expected – I was making a film about dog breeding. I filmed this dog being born and I remember thinking, "I'm not getting one, it's too soon." Before I knew it, I had a puppy. She was always off down the field being independent from the others, so she had all the helpful traits.'

Anyone who has ever gone to visit a litter of puppies 'just to have a look' will empathise. Einich rolled around joyfully on the ground and then shook the dust off. A small boy laughed and tried to hug her. Matt Nightingale, a handler who had just graded with his dog, a short-haired tri-coloured collie, wandered over to speak to me. 'We've just become a qualified search team,' he explained, proudly. 'Morag is my first rescue dog. It took us three years and three months from when we started. We had to build up what we call the "find sequence". Now she's a bit older and smarter, she doesn't always bark the first time at the body – she comes back to find me first. But she always tells me she's found a body.'

At the time I spoke to him, Matt and Morag hadn't been out on any rescues together yet, but he was looking forward to it. He said he's never apprehensive in the mountain rescue. The dogs get called out regularly – twenty calls between January and May. Not all of the dogs used by search and rescue teams are bought and bred for the purpose of training. Matt explained:

'I wanted a puppy to train as a search dog from a reputable breeder but I got her from a rescue shelter instead. She's a rescued rescue dog! She's five now and was two when she started. We were her fourth home. At eighteen months she'd

already been to three homes. Her former owner said she was
always escaping, she had a reputation for running off. But she
has always come back to me on the fells.'

Months later, I remember the bay and pant of the Lake District
rescue dogs on the hills as I lie quietly and wait for a different dog
– Scout – to find me. It seems eerily quiet. I consider what would
happen if I was never found. Would I just stay here obediently,
long past dark? Would I call for help? At Christmas a few years
ago, I went to spend some time in north-west Scotland on my
own, a tiny cottage nestled between Ullapool and Gairloch.
Towards the end of the trip, my friend Andrew came to join me
for a walk. He'd been working in Belgium but was back for a few
days to visit family. As we set out for the hills, I realised he was
driving on the right-hand side of the road, used to European
travel. It took me some time to say anything and – as I hesitated –
I thought about how very British it would be to die of politeness,
to be killed because of a failure to speak up, to risk offending
someone by pointing out a mistake.

Down here in the ground, I think of Charles Foster and his book
*Being a Beast*, his attempt to live as different animals. The book is
more than eccentricity – it's a supreme act of empathy, an attempt
at inhabiting 'the other'. Foster believes that the way we've separated
our world from that of animals is somewhat artificial and masks a
fundamental connection between species:

> What's an animal? It's a rolling conversation with the land from
> which it comes and of which it consists. What's a human? It's a
> rolling conversation with the land from which it comes and of

which it consists – but a more stilted, stuttering conversation than that of most wild animals. The conversations can become stories and acquire the shape and taste of personality. Then they become the sort of animals we celebrate, and the sort of people we want to sit next to at dinner.[23]

Foster set out to spend time as an otter, a red deer, a fox and a swift, occupying different territories on each occasion. In order to try to live as a badger, Foster and his young son Tom ate earthworms and tunnelled into the land to build their very own sett:

We shaped it with our paws and with a child's beach spade (ideal for working in small spaces). We tried to scuffle out the earth with our hind legs but couldn't, because the ceiling was authentically low (most setts are roughly semicircular in profile, being wider than they're high). Tom could pull the bracken bedding in backwards, like proper badgers always do, but it was too much for me. And we sneezed: constantly, mightily and unbadgerishly ... [24]

I'm usually claustrophobic, afraid of lifts, busy theatres and confined spaces. But in my temporary burrow or crouching-place, I feel safe. I feel – I realise – more like a dog. I wonder if part of 'bodying' is also about empathy, about being closer to our animal selves. Perhaps the volunteers at SARDA do this partly through altruism but partly through yearning, a need to feel briefly and brilliantly close to the land. I spoke to a woman in my local climbing shop who regularly volunteers as a 'body' for the dogs, and she described going out to hide on a freezing day but feeling cosier than she ever had. And perhaps there's something strangely 'animal' about being a dog handler too, about training your dog to search and recover. To really be in tune with your canine teammate, perhaps you have to think and be more animal.

I first met beautiful border collie Scout and his handler Paul on a grey Sheffield day. We walked to the Buckstone on Stanage and I scrambled on top of it for joy, slithering down the other side. Scout immediately saw some sheep, his ears pricked up and then he glanced at Paul. Something invisible passed between them and he knew not to go near.

Paul has been walking in the Peak District since he was fourteen. He grew up in Rotherham and comes from industry. He's now studying creative writing at Sheffield Hallam University.

> 'I was an engineer. I left and became a salesman. I was very good at that. Then I woke up one day in a hotel in Frankfurt and said, "OK, I've had enough." Walked out and started a bathroom and kitchen company the next day. I retired when I was forty-seven. In 2012, I'd gone climbing on Dow Crags on Valentine's Day. It was very windy, ice around. In the afternoon, I walked over to the Old Man of Coniston and was planning to drop down. There was a snow cornice on the path so I backtracked. The last thing I can remember is stepping over a brook. Next thing, I woke up in the snow. There was snow on my head and it was red. My scalp had been peeled back. I managed to raise the alarm and mountain rescue came and got me. I was in a very bad way. I was supposed to be going out with my partner and she phoned me while I was still with the mountain rescue to

find out when I was coming home. I'd broken my wrist, my ankle, my legs, smashed my teeth, my ribs ... I had a cup of tea and some cake. To this day I don't know what happened. It took them three and a half hours to get me off. The following February, I went out and did the walk again and then I applied to join mountain rescue – it was a way of giving back.'

He joined the Woodhead branch of mountain rescue as soon as he could. Last time we had a bad snowfall in Sheffield, I opened a copy of *The Independent* and found a report about lorry drivers rescued from their vehicles in the Woodhead Pass. The man they'd interviewed was Paul – he'd been instrumental in their recovery. Paul is modest to a fault in the way he describes himself:

'I'm not a crag rat. I'm what mountain rescue call a donkey – I lug stuff up hills. But I'm good at nav, good at search and rescue, and I just became interested in how the dogs worked. I'm a bit of a loner and that's a thing you need with the dogs. I don't know what it is but we all are.'

As I know from talking to people like Rob Grange, you have to be in a mountain rescue team for at least eighteen months before you can train a dog. But you also have to body first, completing a minimum of ten days nationally. The bodies are the most important thing in the whole of SARDA, Paul argues. Each dog requires a different interaction and response and the bodies must know how to read that. Paul describes the relationship between him and Scout as an experience of 'being at one'. Scout was meant to go to the Swiss Mountain Rescue but Paul ended up with him instead. The dog he had originally planned to have and picked out from a litter ended up as a pet for someone else instead because the breeder reckoned he would be no good for Paul's purposes.

> 'The tragedy would be for him to not grade because of me ... we had a problem where he wouldn't leave me for a bit. It went on for four or five months. I was close to tears, really choked up about it. It gets a lot of the handlers like that. It's such a close bond.'

Paul almost seems tearful whenever he talks about the stresses of training Scout. His social media feed is full of their training adventures and skirmishes together – images of Paul with his legs savaged by brambles, images of Scout lying contented in the bracken, his tongue lolling from the side of his mouth. Beneath this all, I suspect, is the urge to 'be more dog'. In André Alexis's exuberant and surreal novel *Fifteen Dogs*, the question of whether dogs are happier than humans is explored in complex and subtle ways. The book opens with gods Apollo and Hermes having a drink at the Wheat Sheaf Tavern in Toronto's High Park (as well the gods might). Discussing humanity, they begin to argue and end up agreeing a wager. Give animals human intelligence, Apollo claims, and they'll end up even more unhappy than humans are. Hermes isn't so sure. The two gods happen to be near a veterinary clinic where fifteen dogs are being kennelled overnight – handy subjects for their grand experiment. As the novel unfolds, the dogs experience melancholy, confusion and grief (as well as various kinds of unexpected joy). It's a complex novel, difficult to caricature, but one reading of it involves the implication that we'd all be happier if we were less self-aware, less socially tortured, less bound by conventions and rules. In short, we'd all be happier if we were more like dogs. When Paul watches Scout, I sense part of him is running through the bracken too, flirting with the idea of not coming back right away.

'I love him. I really, really love him. It's difficult for me to imagine him not being here. He knows what I require now, can almost read what I want him to do. He'll range up to 300 metres. He might end up on top of a ridge, get a good scent and come all the way back. I trust him and he trusts me.'

I once asked Paul if his relationship with Scout is different from the other dogs he's owned and he agreed right away. Paul is writing a White Peak hiking guidebook and Scout comes on all of his walks.

'He features in the book. The White Peak is more of a human landscape than the Dark Peak, more farms around. It's just like having a walking companion. I've spent time teaching him how to jump over stiles and gates so I don't need to open them. I don't walk with anybody else, just my dog. I've got a photograph of us above Bakewell. We've stopped for lunch and we're under these trees by a little stream. He's had some lunch and he's asleep and I'm sat there and it's just magical. It's everything you want.'

Paul showed me the photo. Dog and owner content in the same purpose, together but slightly apart. There's something very compelling about that slight distance – the way a dog doesn't place demands on you as a human would, doesn't narrate its own experience in familiar language. The needs of dogs seem so simple, so practical, so exact. But perhaps that's just because we don't fully understand them. And perhaps we don't want to, preferring the illusion that we can be small gods to them, provide them with the things they need for comfort and safety. In the image, Paul and Scout look into the same vastness:

> 'It's like two craftsmen working together on the same project and they know what each one is going to be doing. They trust implicitly that each of them will do their own bit. It's more than friends, although he's not a cuddler; he's too independent for that. He's not bothered about being round us in the house, but as soon as he sees the signs of rucksack, lead and boots he's alert.'

Two craftsmen, each reading the other and responding. From my small burrow, I wonder what it must be like to be Scout, free and tethered out on the moor, brought back by an invisible thread.

*Since this chapter was completed, Scout has passed his training and is now a fully qualified Search and Rescue Dog, helping Paul on mountain rescue call-outs whenever he's needed. Scout took some time out from his busy working life to pose for the cover of this book. He was an excellent model.*

# Easedale

The road to Easedale slips out of Grasmere like someone leaving a room without ceremony – there is little traffic, just the determined rise of the tarmac, the youth hostel on the right-hand side, the cottages with their gates to keep out deer. I am short of breath and I slow to a jog, cursing my lack of fitness. The dogs strain on their leads. Soon, we reach the point where the road ends, becoming a private track, and we turn off across a bridge crossing Easedale Beck. There's a small gate and then the valley path becomes slick cobblestones, strangely precarious. There are sheep in the field so I can't let Bell and Charlie go just yet. I notice that Bell is level with me, even slightly in front, not cringing by my heels as she used to. Every so often, she turns to look at me, her tongue hanging out.

The village we have left behind is almost empty. This is a strange, transition season in Grasmere, the end of summer when the tourists disperse, the shops and car parks empty out, the pub is full of familiar faces again. I've come to know how the place shifts, how it is gridlocked in July and August, dead in January. The haunted time is after Christmas when even the hotels shut down. Nobody is buying Grasmere gingerbread. The rowing boats at Faeryland are moored up and still, the swans taking the lake back for themselves. The bag shop is shut up with its endless display of woven carriers locked behind glass, each emblazoned with a trite message: CHOCOLATE IS GOOD. WINE IS GOOD. BAGS ARE GOOD. Last winter, I met the hotel workers who hide invisible in the basement accommodation of The Wordsworth and The Gold Rill, a young couple from Slovakia who have worked here for years and never had time off to see the Lake District hills properly. In January, they appear in the cafes and at the bus stops, unacknowledged and unthanked.

We take the kissing gate on to the fell and begin to climb more steeply beside Sour Milk Gill. It's a peculiar, apt name. The water looks curdled as it falls over stones, tumbles towards Grasmere. The few trees are bold with rust. There's something about autumn that sets me on edge, makes my mind tick faster than usual, like the broken chain on an accelerating bicycle. I want to stand in carpets of leaves, grab clumps of their brittle hair. In the Irish poet Derek Mahon's poem 'Leaves', he describes them as 'prisoners of infinite choice', blown by the wind. He evokes the way they 'scratch like birds at the windows' or move – seemingly unbidden – along the road:

> Somewhere there is an afterlife
> of dead leaves,
> a forest filled with an infinite
> rustling and sighing.
>
> Somewhere in the heaven
> of lost futures
> the lives we might have led
> have found their own fulfilment.[25]

The last stanza of that poem always takes my breath away. It feels natural and extraordinary at the same time, descending from nowhere. It's like the livid sunset you see when you turn a corner, crest the brow of a hill and drive into it astonished. Autumn always makes me feel like a 'prisoner of infinite choice', excited and overwhelmed by the season's possibilities, even as the fallen leaves are meant to symbolise waning and decay. It must be something to do with the 'new term feeling' those of us who work in academia still feel as adults, the rhythm of the year, the way it recalls school days. Early September, when you'd pack a new case full of pencils, unfold the white field of an exercise book, wear uncomfortable shoes, sit next to someone different in class.

It's strange that I should taste excitement in autumn when I used to dread the return to school as a kid. Going back to the routine of the playground and dining hall meant trying to block out the taunts of other children, private lunch breaks by the AstroTurf or eating my sandwiches surreptitiously in the toilets. Even at primary school, I was teased for keeping my head down and blushing when I was asked a question, for not having a strong enough Chesterfield accent. In Year 6, a boy in my class overheard me calling my mum 'Mummy' and cackled in delight and the babyishness of it. A group of kids circled round me at afternoon break, chanting 'Mummy and Daddy' while I tried to escape.

As a teenager, things got worse. I was so lean from distance running that the lads started calling me 'Harold', joking about how I had 'no tits'. My bookishness made me a teacher's pet. I befriended a dreamy girl who suffered from epilepsy and had classroom support for her dyslexia, and I was bullied all the more for hanging round with her. I began spending as much time as

I could between lessons in the library, picking up books I'd read before, trying to engross myself in pictures. I read about the world's largest spiders and the most deadly snakes. Books that took me far from Chesterfield were best. When it was time to go home and face the school bus where boys jeered and whooped and pinched my arse through the seats to make me jump, I wished I had a guard dog next to me, a pit bull or Rottweiler with bunched muscles under its coat that would snap and snarl. It seems strange now to have been so afraid of dogs and yet so drawn to the idea of my own personal canine bodyguard.

As we veer away from the wall, I check for sheep a final time and then I let the dogs go. Charlie hares off into the distance, surprising a group of walkers ahead on the path. His back legs are powerful, his raspberry-coloured tongue lolling from his jaws. His ears are pinned back. Bell trots beside me, checking anxiously for my whereabouts, half running and half walking. The path flattens briefly and narrows and gives some respite, the view opening up. I pass juniper and ferns. I can see out towards Tarn Crag and Blea Rigg. Behind them, the landscape gathers itself, marching towards Langdale. Sergeant Man. Harrison Stickle. Pavey Ark. Knowing they are there is enough. Bell almost trips over her own legs and I almost trip over her. Charlie is well ahead. Then, in an instant, something in her body changes. Something loosens in her bony shoulders and her slim legs. Her jaw seems to relax. The beaten silver of the tarn comes into view and Bell begins to run properly. She is a gathering patch of darkness against the grey sky, smaller as she grows distant and yet somehow magnified in size. I think of the greyhounds I saw once at Owlerton stadium in Sheffield, how their first movements from the traps seemed snatched before they found their easy rhythm, how their legs would open up and snap shut as they cornered the track. Bell is like that now. She does not care where I am; she is galloping into the open, her sturdy, slender body propelling her up the hill towards the water. For the first time, she does not look back. There is something elastic about her movements. Soon, she has caught Charlie, and for a moment they hare along beside each other, pace for pace. At the tarn, I catch up with them and they are all shuddering flanks and concertina ribcages, attentive and bright with effort. We cross at the mouth of the tarn and begin the descent from Upper Easedale, freewheeling down towards a huge boulder. Bell continues to run free.

I spend the next few weeks in the small park with my friend Jan and both dogs. My favourite game is to get Jan to hold on to Bell's collar while I sprint a few hundred metres across the grass. Then he lets her go and I turn in time to see her thundering towards me. She has found a brief freedom. In the house, she still whimpers and whines when I try to leave her, but out in the crisp, rotten-apple-and-dew air she has her independence. I remember how it felt when I started walking home from school. At lunch-times, the lads had taken to lifting me up by my feet and arms and depositing me in a bin behind the sports block. My lunchbox cracked in my bag. Wasps buzzed around my hair and face. That day, I left as soon as the bell rang and instead of turning left towards the buses, turned right through the huge gates. My breathing slowed down the hill towards Hady. But when I reached the track near Dark Lane, I let myself run, bag bouncing around awkwardly on my back.

# Hauntings

I'm sleeping out on a rock for the first time. 'Rock' isn't quite right. It's more like a gnarled wisdom tooth. 'Sleep' isn't right either. Each time I open my eyes, I'm startled by the stars above Tilberthwaite quarry, expecting the curtained dark of my room and not this almost living brightness. The sky seems incredibly close to my face. I feel bones in my body I've never noticed before. Beside me, the two whippets have curled themselves tight against the cold. They're so still I have to keep pressing my hands against their sides to check they're breathing. This is the nearest I'll probably get to bivvying on a mountain. Bivvying without the stonefall, altitude and risk.

Why did I stay? Looking round, I can only just distinguish the thicker darkness of rocks from the less substantial dark of the grass. Tilberthwaite is a natural amphitheatre, high on the hill not far from Coniston. An old slate quarry. We limped up to it from the car park that afternoon, me and two friends, struggling under the fog of last night's whisky. Dusk had got to Tilberthwaite before us, but we'd set up ropes anyway.

Rock climbing in half-light is absorbing – angling your face so your head torch vaguely whitens the space in front of you, then trusting your feet. Once that evening, when I paused after clipping in, looked down from midway up the slab, the light was playing tricks on me: I thought I saw a huge, brown dog run into the quarry and out again. A kind of giant lurcher. It had no collar and it moved with an elegance that didn't suit a dog of its size. Then, it was gone. There was nothing below except my friend Ben holding the rope, a few sheep grazing the sparse grass and my own dogs, tethered to a tree.

We climbed until it was getting too dark to see our own fingers, then made a fire from the huge branches and smaller, dry twigs gathered from a copse. Nobody had a knife. Scott and Ben had to use one branch as a kind of seesaw until they cracked it and fell to the floor in a heap. I'd found an unreliable lighter in my pocket, the pale blue one I used to light other people's cigarettes. Scott built a small circle out of slates and stones, a miniature drystone wall to protect the flames, and, eventually, we'd settled down, drinking warm Corona. For the first time in a year, I felt a kind of peace, entertained the idea that nothing existed beyond this quarry, this circle of faint light.

But lying on my ledge in the middle of the night, I can't see our stones any more. The wind is doing its rounds, inspecting the corners of the quarry and me in the centre of it. I could have gone back to the car when the fire went out and the others started packing up. Even now, I could trust my head torch, pick my way through the pitch blackness, start the engine and drive back to my house. Couldn't I? No. I don't dare move. I've no idea why. All I can do is lie on my back, listening, looking up at the terrifying stars, as if I've become part of the quarry floor.

I think about the same things I always do at 4 a.m. when I'm sleepless in bed. I imagine waking up in every room I used to live in. I remember the field at the bottom of my parents' house in Chesterfield, the view from my old bedroom window at night.

All the time, I'm aware of each small movement in the quarry. I sense something padding nearby, and wonder if it's the brown lurcher, if I'd really seen it after all. I imagine footsteps, too loud to be animal, too soft to be human.

Most, I think of Shackleton, how, moving through South Georgia, exhausted, he thought there must be four men in their party, not three. Reinhold Messner reported the same sensation in the mountains, after losing his brother in an accident. It's the sense John Burnside describes in his poem 'The Good Neighbour', the idea of another being drawing close, mirroring your own movements.[26]

I wonder who my ghost companion would be. There are countless ghost stories and superstitious tales set in the amphitheatres of mountains – a girl seen dancing near the summit of Moel Famau, a large grey man supposed to haunt the slopes of Ben Macdui, the ghost army that marches across Souther Fell in Cumbria. Cader Idris in Wales is so steeped in myth and legend that it's said that anyone who spends the night there alone will either die, become insane or become a poet (some might say that's the same thing). Unsurprisingly, many mountain ghost stories also feature spectral hounds.

Perhaps the most famous of these is the legend of Gelert the faithful hound, believed to stalk the Aberglaslyn Pass in Snowdonia. In the thirteenth century, Prince Llywelyn the Great had a palace at Beddgelert in Caernarfonshire, and he spent much of his time in the surrounding countryside with his pack of hunting dogs. One day when he summoned the hounds as usual with his horn, his favourite dog Gelert didn't appear, so regretfully Llywelyn had to set out without him. When Llywelyn returned from the hunt, he was greeted by Gelert who came bounding towards him, jaws dripping with blood. The Prince was seized with the sudden terror that the blood might belong to his infant son. He burst into the child's nursery, only to find the baby missing and the walls smeared with blood. Grief-maddened, he turned on Gelert – the only possible murderer – and plunged a sword through the dog's heart. But as the dog howled his last, Llywelyn heard his son wail from underneath his upturned cradle. Beside him was a dead wolf. The horrible truth of the situation dawned on the Prince: Gelert had protected the boy, not killed him. To this day, a cairn marks the spot where Llywelyn buried Gelert so that everyone could see the grave of his brave and loyal animal, slain in error. It's said that Gelert still roams around Snowdonia, mournful after death.

The sinisterly named Hanging Hills of south central Connecticut in the USA are also thought to be home to a supernatural hound. They're a range of mountainous trap-rock ridges overlooking the city of Meriden and the Quinnipiac River Valley and popular with outdoor adventurers. But they're also frequented by a small black dog which leaves no trace of its presence: no footprints and no sound. If you see the black dog once, it might be perfectly innocuous – in fact, a first sighting is believed to result in joy. Seeing the dog a second time, however, signifies a warning. And if you see the dog for a third time, it's an omen of death. In February 1891, geologists Herbert Marshall and W.H.C. Pynchon were conducting a geological survey in the Hanging Hills when the dog appeared on the horizon. Pynchon had seen this apparition once before and Marshall had seen it twice. He scoffed at the idea of it signifying doom and they carried on with their work. But shortly afterwards, Marshall slipped on ice and plunged to his death from a clifftop. At least six deaths in the Hanging Hills have now been blamed on third sightings of the elusive black dog.

In her book *Explorers of the Infinite*, Maria Coffey argues that the survival of extreme adventurers depends on a kind of hypervigilance, an extreme awareness of their surroundings. They're constantly monitoring their sensory world – the rough texture of rock under their fingers, how their crampons bite into the ice, the temperamental shifts in weather. They might be required to respond to danger and react quickly at any point:

> Their lives depend upon this process – what some psychologists call 'thin slicing' – of finding patterns in situations and behaviour based on very narrow segments of experience. It's what most of us call intuition, a 'knowing without knowing'.[27]

Coffey found herself wondering whether becoming so closely attuned to the natural world leads to mountaineers and other extreme adventurers opening 'channels to hidden powers and realms of experience that we call mystical and paranormal'.[28] Does risk-taking lead to a kind of spiritual hypersensitivity, a tendency to see things that other people might not?

The phenomenon of a phantom climbing partner has been reported by early Himalayan mountaineers and by more recent expeditions alike. On the famous 1924 Everest expedition, Howard Somervell heard human voices warning his party to go 'thus far and no further'. Other members of early expeditions hallucinated strange crosses, colours and unfamiliar sounds.

In 1988, British mountaineer Stephen Venables became the first person to ascend Everest by the Kangshung Face. When he was forced to spend a night close to the summit, he was joined by an elderly man who encouraged him to descend to the South Summit, exhausted and stumbling. Stranger still, when Venables reached the South Summit, he encountered the spirit of dead explorer Eric Shipton who helped to warm up his hands after his ordeal. In 1983, Australian climber Greg Child and his partner Pete Thexton were on Broad Peak in Pakistan when Pete became seriously ill. As he carried his friend down the mountain, Child was convinced he was being guided by a presence just behind him.

This 'friendly spirit' echoes the experience of couple Lou and Ingrid Whittaker on Kanchenjunga in 1989. At base camp, Lou became convinced that there was a middle-aged Tibetan woman in his tent, a benign presence in traditional dress. His wife Ingrid was also on the mountain and after descending to base camp with altitude sickness, she had to rest in Lou's tent. While Lou was out climbing, Ingrid was sure that she was kept company by the shadowy presence of a local woman who placed a hand on her forehead to soothe the terrible headaches she was experiencing. In 2018, French climber Élisabeth Revol reported something similar on Nanga Parbat in Pakistan during a violent storm. After having to leave her climbing partner Tomek Mackiewicz behind for dead, Revol had made her way down the Kinshofer route to a crevasse where she spent the night. 'I imagined people were bringing me hot tea,' she told *The Guardian*. 'A woman asked me if in return she could take my shoe. At that moment, I automatically got up, took off my shoe and gave it to her. In the morning when I woke up, I was only in my sock.'[29]

Hallucinations are much more common above 28,000 feet. Scientists at the Laboratory of Cognitive Neuroscience in Switzerland in Lausanne have suggested that exposure to altitude affects the temporoparietal junction and the prefrontal cortex of the brain, perhaps leading to prefrontal lobe dysfunctions (commonly found during ecstatic religious experiences). Other explanations for the effects include a kind of temporal lobe epilepsy. Maria Coffey reports the work of Canadian psychiatrist Robert Persinger, who developed a helmet that would shoot electric currents into specific areas of the brain to create micro-seizures. Aiming these currents at the temporal lobes would often lead to subjects reporting 'spectral presences'. Since the left hemisphere of the temporal cortex is reported to be the home of our 'sense of self', scientists like Persinger believe that such presences are actually a transient awareness of the right hemi-spheric equivalent of the left hemispheric sense of self. This connects to the work of neuroscientists like V.S. Ramachandran on visions and apparitions, which he argues are projections of the body and mind. Our body image, Ramachandran believes, is an internal construct which can be manipulated. In one experiment, Ramachandran would sit at a table with a volunteer who had one hand hidden from view under the tabletop. Ramachandran would then simultaneously tap the surface of the table and the volunteer's hidden hand. Many volunteers reported feeling the tapping not in their hand but within the table itself, a strange experience apparently outside the boundaries of the body.

Yet some of these neuroscientific explanations ('a transient awareness of the right hemispheric equivalent of the left hemispheric sense of self') sound almost as mysterious as the

visions of climbers themselves. Maria Coffey remains uncon-
vinced by rational dismissals. Before writing her book, she says,
she was 'on the fence' about paranormal or spiritual experiences:

> What stopped me from settling firmly on the side of rationalism
> were memories of puzzling incidents in my life – a mystical
> 'awakening' after I nearly drowned off the coast of Morocco;
> a premonition of my lover's death on Everest and the
> 'visitations' I received from him after the news was confirmed;
> the spirit of a river that protected me from illness and banditry
> while I kayaked hundreds of miles down its course. At the time,
> I'd rationalised each of these sensations as being the result of
> fear, worry, grief or exhaustion. But listening to the stories of
> adventurers made me wonder if, perhaps, they were more than
> just products of my imagination.[30]

In the quarry, I can hear breath right next to my ear. Animal
breath. When I turn my face towards it, there's no heat. Why
should a ghostly dog be a bad omen, I wonder? A dog – real or
imagined – might be a kindly mountain guide. I remember
conversations with fellow writer Ed Douglas where he described
being joined in the mountains ('adopted') by dogs who followed
him, once in Tibet ('it's like the mountains know you need
a friend') and once near the Georgian border in the Kaçkar
mountains. In one of Ed's images, a huge sand-coloured dog rolls
on the floor next to his daughter, nuzzling her leg gently with his
snout. The breed are called Kangal dogs and have been bred in
Turkey to protect against wolves. Named after a town in the
southern Sivas province, where Kangals emerged as a distinct

breed about 6,000 years ago, the dogs are bigger than Great Danes – sixty-five kilograms and up to eighty-five centimetres tall. Wolves have been a problem for the thousands of years that Turkey's farmers have been raising sheep in mountainous regions. They tend to attack alone or in pairs, usually in the mornings, and sometimes they've even been known to kill humans too. The very sight of a Kangal dog may be enough to scare away a predator. Their ears are docked to stop wolves from catching hold of them. Their intimidating stature and guard-dog efficiency have begun to make them a popular currency beyond Turkey: breeders in Western Montana have imported the dogs since 2009. An *Outside* article by Stephen Starr reported American farmer Vose Babstock on the breed: 'They can fight off a wolf, mountain lion or bear and then come home and be polite with grandparents and grandchildren.'[31] To be joined by one of these gentle giants in the hills must have been a humbling experience. In the photo Ed sent to me, the Kangal looks like a gleeful puppy sunbathing.

Back in Tilberthwaite, there's no further sign of the spectral hound. As I lie without moving in the quarry, listening to the breath of my sleeping dogs, I realise it isn't the idea of other living things that scares me; it's the idea that nothing else is here in the dark. That's what I wanted when I decided to stay here – that I'm really alone, just for one night. I think about the morning not arriving – this being normal. I think about it constantly until the moment when, at last, a violet kind of light bleeds into the quarry, gives the boulders back their shapes and finds me on my small ledge, not quite ready to move yet, grateful for the slight sounds of bees at work, this landscape that has tolerated me and, when I'm ready, will let me go.

# Helm Crag

The first time I lose the two dogs, it's a perfectly still afternoon and the light is just fading over the ring of fells to the west of Grasmere. The growing twilight adds to my sense of panic. We climbed up from Helm Crag, scrambling over loose stones, passing the hidden, blocky places where I climbed in summer, dodging falling stones. We passed The Lion and The Lamb, poised anthropomorphised stones on the summit, one looming and one tentative. I carried on to the next peak and the next, hoping to eventually descend to Easedale. It only took a second for them to bolt. There must have been roaming sheep I hadn't seen, or a flash of rabbit – we passed the maggoty carcass of a sheep on the ascent and I had to drag the whippets away by their collars. They took off in the same direction, careering down a sheer slope. Now, I pace and call, pace and call, higher and more insistent each time. I can't even see them, can't even guess which direction they might have travelled in. I whistle through my teeth, as shrill as I can manage. Silence. The caw of a crow. A cow lowing far below.

Elizabeth Bishop's plaintive poem 'One Art' is quoted so often its use has almost become a cliche.[32] In her taut villanelle, she repeatedly asserts that it is not difficult to learn the 'art' of losing. I have always thought of myself as someone comfortable with loss, with change. As an adult, I've rarely stayed in the same house for longer than six months, bundling my belongings in the same borrowed suitcases and half a dozen cardboard boxes and looking for somewhere better. I end relationships before anyone else has chance to, detaching myself quietly and efficiently, ignoring phone calls and demands for an explanation. I throw things away – even letters which have sentimental value – on a whim when my room seems too cluttered. I'm a strange mix of sentimentality and ruthlessness. I've always felt a strange affinity with the narrator in Richard Wilbur's compelling long narrative poem 'The Mind-Reader', a dramatic monologue which centres around a man who feels afflicted with his gift of seeing into other people's thoughts. In the poem, Wilbur evokes the haunted landscape of the mind as a dense forest, full of thickets, difficult to move through.

I've long been fascinated by this image for the way we try to remember, doggedly chasing the lost thing through the undergrowth, under the cold stars. The Mind-Reader in the poem is tired of being able to help people find their lost things, bored with soothing their anxieties. He drinks to forget and longs to escape the persistence of memory. He wishes he could occupy a place where some things are really, truly lost, where even he cannot see them.[33] When I first encountered 'The Mind-Reader', I felt I understood. Knowledge is exhausting. There's a place somewhere towards the bottom of your second pint where you feel content to let go. I've even been able to lose poems and stories in the past, refusing to write them down and accepting that they might drift from my consciousness, the way you wake in the middle of the night from a vivid dream and swear you'll inhabit it until morning, only to find that it has slipped away, leaving the barest imprint.

It's almost dark now. I meet a couple beginning their descent from the hill and they sense my panic, stop to ask what's wrong. When I explain, they help me comb the fellside for a while and when they finally give up and return to their walk, they take my phone number so they can get in touch if they discover the dogs. I almost shake with gratitude. I'm tormenting myself now, thinking of all the times I imagined my life might be easier without Bell's neediness and whimpering, imagining that I might have brought this on myself with the power of my own thoughts. There's a strange arrogance in that idea, something I used to feel as a child when I first became aware of the power of my own mind and – subsequently – first experienced obsessive thoughts and something like depression. I would become fixated on the notion that I must not think about something (sometimes this was a specific thing, sometimes it was the self-conscious awareness of thought itself) and would then drive myself mad for hours because, of course, I'd be unable to get what it was out of my mind. No matter how pleasant the day was and no matter what I was doing, I'd be tormented by the idea that I was thinking banned thoughts. This became my guilty secret. I remember a sunny afternoon in Birmingham with my step-gran and mum where we'd been out to a cafe and walked in the park. We got back to my step-gran's house and I sat on the sofa, surrounded by people who loved me, unable to relax because of my recursive loop of thoughts. I can't have been more than ten or eleven at the time.

When I finally find the dogs, it's almost by accident: I stumble in the fading light and slip a few metres down some scree. There they are, huddled on a ledge, the ground around them so steep they can't move with confidence. They are both trembling and pathetic, looking to me for solace. When they escaped, they were all teeth and bravado. If they were human, I'd expect a humble apology. Somehow, I manage to get to them and coax them down an insufficient path, a bad route back to Easedale. When we reach flatter ground, a drystone wall blocks our way and – exasperated – I end up lifting them over it one by one before scrambling and flopping over myself. I graze my stomach and my ribs and the skin smarts sharply. On the track back into Grasmere, I keep them on a lead even though it seems unnecessary: they are walking slowly now, abashed.

Back in the village, I pass the couple whose kindness on the hill had touched me so deeply. They're in the window of Tweedies, sharing pints and fish and chips. They bang against the glass when they see me and I duck in to thank them again. The man kneels to fuss Bell and Charlie in turn, ruffling Charlie's velvet fur. He wags his tail enthusiastically. Bell is shivering, keen to be home. The woman wags her finger at them and tuts indulgently: 'You've given your mum a real fright.'

They go back into the warmth and I go back into the darkness, ignoring the bar and the greetings from mates who are on duty. On the way back, the dogs spot the white muzzle of a badger and they are animated again, dragging me full pelt into the night as they try to catch up with it. They never do. The badger belongs to a world they can't reach, as private and inaccessible as their world is to me.

# Dog words and gritstone

When I first met Lucy Creamer, Stanage was deserted, the rock cold and reptilian to the touch. We pulled our down jackets tight around us and eyed the bat-coloured sky, anticipating rain. I busied myself with the gear in my rucksack, pretending I wasn't nervous about a trad-climbing lesson with a great climber. A gust from the west threatened to carry my waterproof top away in its grip. Stanage is always so much windier than the towns and valleys around it, cross-hatched by weather. Though the gritstone routes are only short, the difference between the bottom of the routes and the top is extraordinary – I've often belayed in winds so strong I could barely hear myself think, shouting down to my climbing partner and hoping they could hear me. Something about the wildness of it makes you feel like an impostor, teetering on the edge of threat, even though Sheffield always winks close by, even though you always know you could scramble down to safety.

Lucy's reputation goes before her, in the Peak District and beyond. Big, alpine-style routes around the world have always appealed to her and in 2000 she climbed the Hasse Brandler (ED) on Cima Grande in the Dolomites with Airlie Anderson. The year after, a trip to Greenland led to the first ascent of *Venus Envy*, a 600-metre E4/5 on The Baroness. But in the Peak District with a harness full of trad gear, she seems most at home.

That blustery day on Stanage under Lucy's guidance, I led my first HVS or Hard Very Severe route: something unremarkable, short and slightly overhanging near the Popular End that I'd always been scared to try before. It was called *Nothing To Do With Dover*, a name like a wry nod across a crowded pub (all of the other routes on Dover's Wall had utilitarian monikers). What Stanage lacks in height it makes up for in brutality – skin-grazing fist-jams and steep cracks. I'd been trad climbing since I was seventeen, but always at the same beginner's level, always afraid to try things I might fall from. Lucy talked me through every move with patience and confidence. Her large, brindled dog charged around at the foot of the crag. When I hauled myself over the top, panting and elated, I smiled to hear the jangle of the dog's collar and see her bounding towards me. I thought then about the first time I ever climbed outdoors, flailing helplessly on the end of a rope on an easy route called *Flying Buttress*, a day so warm it felt as if the rock itself was sweating. Every move and every small failure filled me with frustration. I remember a collie dancing round the rocks at the top of the route, its master calling in the distance, and how I envied its unencumbered freedom, wondered why I'd tethered myself to a rope in the first place. Climbing with Lucy holding my ropes felt controlled. I didn't dare to make my usual excuses: the cold numbing my fingertips, a lack of gear. She believed I could do it, and so I did. I simply got on with things.

Today, I'm meeting Lucy again inside the red brick walls of Sheffield University's old and imposing Firth Court building, in a coffee shop nestled at the heart of campus. It's a world away from that route. Five years have passed. We both have shorter hair and neither of us is really climbing these days: me because of pregnancy and Lucy because of the demands of the course she's studying for. There's something comforting to me in her acceptance of this, of her willingness to adapt to life changing, her refusal to worship the small and dictatorial god of rock climbing. We drink coffee and talk about shifting responsibility, changing priorities and how a life with dogs might be intrinsic to that. Lucy's face is alert but steady – she has sharp, intelligent features and kind eyes. Her arms are taut and her fingers are quick. I remember her showing me how to do a hand jam properly on Stanage, how to torque my small hand, turn my knuckles so that I could find leverage in cracks in the rock. I feel acutely aware of my new softness now, how my round belly almost touches the table. I switch on my phone recorder and we begin.

Lucy tells me they had family dogs when she was a young teenager and she took responsibility for them. She came from a sporty background but her parents didn't spend a lot of time outdoors with her. Taking the dogs out made her realise that she felt an affinity with the adventures and landscapes she accessed through them. As an adult, Lucy got a dog ten years into her climbing career and says it was more her partner's decision than hers. That decision changed the whole course of her life as an athlete:

> 'You can't just jet off anywhere with a dog ... it did curtail my trad climbing ... I always thought about the dog's needs before my own and I couldn't bring myself to leave it at the top of Gogarth for five hours. It became easier to go sport climbing. So my climbing changed.'

The first time Lucy took her 'street urchin' dog to the Peak District, she came alive and leapt around in the bracken, delirious with joy. She was called Kodo, Japanese for 'heartbeat'. Lucy got her from the RSPCA, a Staffie crossed with a Shar Pei. She had been adopted by a family who brought her back saying she was unmanageable, but they had never actually tried to walk her. Kodo died in 2012 and Lucy has subsequently got two more dogs, a mastiff/boxer cross and a whippet/Staffie cross. Lucy seems less at ease talking about Kodo at first, perhaps because the memories are too raw: 'she was just the most amazing crag dog. I drove all over Europe with her. She would just go off and make friends with people. She was just brilliant.' When she died, Lucy says it was 'horrendous, like losing a child'.

In his moving essay 'An Absence Bounding At Our Side', climber and author Jim Perrin attempts to capture the heartbreak dog owners experience when they lose a pet, appealing even to those who might claim an indifference to dogs:

> You may not like dogs, or even animals at all, and if so, that's your business and I have no desire to criticise. This account may leave you quite cold. My point in writing it is not self-indulgence or maudlin sentimentality but a need to express this: wherever and in whatever sphere our response to the world is predicated on love, we are increased in our dignity of sentient being, and the world is enhanced. If you desire to counter that by pointing out that a love of animals is easy by comparison with love for our fellow human beings or our abused planet, I wouldn't necessarily disagree with you, but questions of degree do not discount the essential point.

Love in its every form, so long as it's possessed at root of a pure and disinterested concern for the other's welfare – whoever or whatever that other may be – is our truest point of connection into the world we inhabit.

Jim's dog was called The Flea and was originally intended as a pet for his son but, inevitably, care soon devolved to the adults. And The Flea became a steadfast outdoor companion from those early days. Jim recalls a walk with her on Kinder Scout in her first winter, in the snow: 'how pitiful she looked and tired she became, sunk through on her short legs to her hairless puppy's belly; and how, wrapped in a duvet jacket, she rode inside my rucksack with her head sticking out; and how always thereafter on the rare occasions when fatigue overtook her or in periods of rest, my rucksack became her habitual nesting place, and its contents would be dragged out by her to make room if necessary.' Jim had always told himself that he didn't like small dogs, their yappiness and their temperamental uncertainties. But he was quickly won over. The Flea appears in his outdoor photographs, scampering into the frame or peering from behind a cairn. She became lithe and hardy: 'on scrambling sections where she couldn't find her own way round she was so light and agile she could be carried, or thrown up steep and difficult bits, and once over them she'd make her way to some vantage point and look down panting with excitement, ready to lick furiously at the first face that might arrive at her ledge.' When Jim appeared on Cameron McNeish's popular *Wilderness Walks* programme, the dog appeared with him and soon began to receive her own fan mail. When The Flea died, Jim had to reconfigure his relationship with mountains and with the outdoors, since so much of it had been filtered through the experience of having a dog:

> Being outdoors with a dog teaches you more alertly to see. It is as simple as that: the hedgehog in the drift of leaves; the other path, branching off through a thicket in the wood, that her instinct hunted out and that led where you wanted to go; the badger sett below the coastal path, all sign of it hidden from above, that her nostrils quivered at; the stalking fox she saw first at Gloywlyn, that a chance move might have sent slinking away. She gave me things to see ... [34]

The way Jim writes about his love for The Flea and the strange way we conceptualise our affection for dogs – a love which seems both complicated and pure – echoes poet Mark Doty's writing in his memoir about his retriever, *Dog Years*. Doty explores how it is possible to love beyond language, opening with the premise 'no dog has ever said a word, but that doesn't mean they live outside the world of speech. They listen acutely ... '.[35] To choose to live with a dog, Doty argues, is to agree to participate in a long process of interpretation, a process which – as Jim Perrin notes – might perhaps seem simpler in the outdoors. As Doty observes, it is always difficult to try to explain your love of someone ('you can describe your beloved until the tongue tires and still, in truth, fail to get at the particular quality that has captured you').[36] This is even more complicated in the case of a pet:

> Maybe the experience of loving an animal is actually more resistant to language, since animals cannot speak back to us,

cannot characterise themselves or correct our assumptions about them. They look at us across a void made of the distance between their lives and our immersion in language. 'Not a single one of his myriad sensations,' wrote Virginia Woolf of Elizabeth Barrett Browning's cocker spaniel Flush, 'ever submitted itself to the deformity of words.'[37]

Sociologist Mariam Motamedi-Fraser has studied the notion of 'dog words', aided by her black Labrador, Monk, who she takes to her office at Goldsmiths University (Monk even has his own staff page and Mariam contends that he behaves differently 'at work' and at rest). Mariam is interested in how words have a life beyond what we generally think of as 'our language' and that we should also attend to the sound, feel, touch, taste, place, position, speed and direction of words, all of which have significance to us. She believes that words can take on a meaning without having first passed through language ('language, one might say, is an obedience trial for words; words in language are words in formal training') and that we can therefore forge new 'words' through our intimate relationship to dogs. How can a dog speak? Dogs make 'dog words' with their bodies, just as a spoken word is made by the sound that is shaped by the face, mouth, larynx, etc. and a written word is made by the movement of the hand and the marker. She argues that there are similarities in the development of children and dogs, both of whom group kinds of word together because of perceived commonalities between them. Mariam goes even further, suggesting that dogs perhaps have a fuller relationship to language than the one we have: 'For me, a dog always means what she says because the meaning of a dog word is always arrived at by way of a particular encounter. Somewhat counter-intuitively, this specificity – of relations and modes of relationality – gives dog words a greater pliability than is available to words in language.'[38] Surely the gestural, physical language that can exist between dogs and their owners is heightened in the mountains, in situations where the two communicate outdoors.

Mark Doty suggests that – in the different language they use – perhaps dogs remind us of our own origins, a time 'when our bodies were not yet assumed into the world of speech'. He continues:

> Then we could experience wordlessly, which must at once be a painful thing and a strange joy, a pure kind of engagement that adults never know again ... we suffer a loss, leaving the physical world for the world of words – even though we gain our personhood in the process.[39]

Perhaps Doty has a slightly different conception of the way dogs relate to 'words' than the model suggested by Mariam Motamedi-Fraser, but they both agree that communication between humans and animals can seem a form of 'enchantment', physical and environmental, ever changing. Lucy Creamer's new dogs just don't have the same relationship with her and with the mountains as Kodo did. She clearly loves them, but the connection isn't as intimate – you might say they share less of a gestural and physical language. Attempts to take the whippet-Staffie to Europe have been less successful ('I was meant to be out there for months. I nearly came back after the first week. He just wanted to kill every dog at first sight. We were on narrow ledges where he had no escape.

I nearly had to muzzle him.'). Most of her memorable experiences of taking dogs to mountains involve Kodo. Lucy recounted doing a classic E6 in Devon, a few pitches, with her beloved first dog left at the top. 'This horrific thunderstorm came in. We were climbing under a massive roof and we could see it coming in across the sea. It began to hammer with rain, thunder and lightning. I couldn't do anything about the dog. I was just glad I hadn't tied her up.' When they topped out, Lucy's dog wasn't there. 'I got a phone call – she had found a cafe and they were looking after her with a bed and feed! She was totally fine. I have no idea how she got there – it was half a mile away. She'd obviously been traumatised by the lightning but she was a true survivor, went and found people and got looked after.'

Lucy's story makes me remember the guilt I experienced when I tied my two whippets to a post at the bottom of an undemanding route in Langdale, just behind the Old Dungeon Ghyll pub. I'd thought we'd reach the top in no time – three pitches, easy climbing, unthreatening weather – but my climbing partner was hung-over from a house party the night before, the kind where you wake up in a bathtub full of empty beer cans. He floundered with the belays. I made heavy weather of the route-finding, the slippery and polished holds. As we got higher and began to inch out of view, the dogs began to howl with anguish. I regretted tying them up, but couldn't have trusted them off-lead amongst sheep and scuttling rabbits. Perhaps I was being punished for my lack of faith. Every whimper and bark went through me, made me place my feet more uncertainly. Afterwards, some men climbing a nearby route posted a complaint about the dogs on an online forum, lamenting how the barking had distracted them. My guilt turned to irrational anger then, as if I were being criticised myself, as if their distressed sounds had escaped from my own body. Lucy is stoical about the moulding effect dogs have had on her climbing and her life:

> 'I've learned a lot from dogs. They're very patient, which I'm not, and they seem to just accept things, accept situations. The dogs I have now are really good like that, not questioning. I'm not saying that's something you should do all the time, but I've learned something from how they approach things.'

I think about Bell and the unwavering faith she seemed to have in me when we walked together in Cumbria, how distressing it was when she apparently lost that faith the moment I tried to leave her in the house. Though she seemed to fail at acceptance (never believing that I would come back) I realised that I struggled with it too: I wanted a dog, but I wasn't prepared for how much my life might have to change with the needs of a damaged rescue animal who couldn't be left. I needed to change my life, but I was unwilling, stubbornly hoping that I could improve her capacity to be alone. Lucy recognises the shift towards – perhaps unwanted – responsibility that a dog can engender:

> 'I suppose I was a very impulsive person before I got dogs, I'd do things on a whim ... planning has become more of a feature of my life, I've had to be more organised with my time. But I've also learned to be in the moment a bit more. They're not looking ahead or thinking about the past, they're in the moment. I don't do that enough. My brain's always working at ninety miles an hour.'

Now that she's studying at Sheffield University and her time is scarce, Lucy often chooses dogs over climbing. 'I would have done a lot more trad climbing if I hadn't had dogs. I love spending time with them. At the moment, if I have time I want to take them into the Peak. We feed off each other in those environments.' I find this refreshing. As someone who has often fallen in and out of love with trad rock climbing, going out obsessively some years and then avoiding the gritstone for months at a time, it seems reassuring that a climber like Lucy could put her sport to the side at times, accept other priorities. There's a necessary unselfishness about dog ownership, we both agree. I find myself talking to Lucy about some of my anxieties around having a child. My due date is fast approaching and I haven't felt able to tell people how I stir restlessly in the night, worrying about the responsibility, trying to visualise a crib next to my bed, hopefully imagining myself walking up Mam Tor with the child in a backpack or sling in wintertime, but secretly fearing that I might not be able to take off into the hills with him, that my body or mind will fail me, that I'll be housebound, trapped with the cornices and green chimneys of my own mind. When I first got a dog, I loved her unconditionally but I also resented her at times. Are children so different?

Lucy listens to me calmly. We wonder together whether sometimes people take on dogs as a means of deliberately limiting themselves, because it's the right time for that level of responsibility. The excuse to leave the party. The reason to disappear. When I lived in the Lake District, I would often find myself using Bell's nervousness as an excuse to go home when I was feeling particularly anxious. Lucy pauses:

'It's complicated. When we first got Kodo, I found it really hard
to accept having her and having to curtail my lifestyle at that
point. It was hard making that adjustment but I think it wasn't
a bad thing and I think it contributed to me being more con-
structive with my time. I'd just never had any routine before.'

Driving down into Hathersage recently to meet Jon and Polly for
a walk to the millpond, I caught a feature on Radio 4 about how
women make the decision about whether or not they should
have children. An American life coach was explaining how she
counsels women through their dilemmas, encouraging them to
think about their lifestyles, hopes, fears and aspirations, how a
family might impact on all of these. At the end of the programme,
some example questions were given: does the thought of mother-
hood fill you with a sense of heaviness and responsibility? I flinched
a little in my seat. Of course, I thought. I'm weeks away from
giving birth and I feel like that. But it doesn't take away the
impulse to love and care for a child. Perhaps if I'd been to see a
life coach, I would have been convinced that I didn't want
children at all. Perhaps I would have been convinced never to
adopt a dog.

Some decisions are made with our bodies, or our lives seem to
make them for us. They are more like the next move on a gritstone
climb than a deliberate route choice on a walk, a decision to
continue or turn back. And for some, the choice never exists at
all. Lucy and I are both agreed that dogs have appeared in our
lives outdoors in ways that seemed both deliberate but strangely
inevitable. And though I sense her current dogs can never offer
her the intimate climbing experiences she had with Kodo, they

offer unconditional love, a sense of enjoyment in the Peak District that becomes infectious. Dogs, we agree, can convince you to get out of the door. Lucy smiles as I switch off my recorder:

'Dogs don't fake it. What you see is what you get.'

# Fairfield

It's only just gone 5 a.m. when I pull up beside the church at Rydal and leave the car in gear on the hill. Thin birdsong. The sunlight is hard on the fellside, too bright to be buttery – a promise of expected morning, unseasonal warmth. There's nobody else here yet. The dogs don't get out of the back immediately when I open the door for them – it's too early; I had to coax them from bed. They usually start as soon as they see my fell-running shoes or hear the sound of the zip on my windproof jacket. They follow obediently, grudgingly, and we start to walk up the steep slope past Rydal Hall. As we get through the gate, I unleash them and we start to run.

There's a man I know in the village who comes out with a head torch to jog the Fairfield Horseshoe every time he's suffering from insomnia. He's wiry, precise and cheerful. Sixteen kilometres and 1,048 metres of ascent. I imagine him moving, swift and sleepless, returning to Ambleside before anyone else is awake, shaking his limbs off and drinking black coffee in the yard outside his house. I've only been here once before and it was to walk with friends, hung-over and groggy from a beer festival in the village. I didn't have dogs then. We had brought no water, no food. The route was longer than we thought, the views finer. Somewhere, there's a photograph of me standing on top of Fairfield and looking into the mist, my friend Chris crouched down on a rock beside me.

In the image, we are just shapes, no more than trees and boulders. I like the anonymity of it, my face turned away towards Windermere, the silver and the houses below.

The climb to Nab Scar from Rydal Bridge is snaking, punishing. My thighs are already burning and, instead of a run, I'm reduced to walking with my hands pressed down on the top of my legs. The dogs canter behind, tongues lolling. When I pause to turn, I can see the shape of Rydal Water like a speech bubble. My lungs are full of heat. I imagine my ribs as the bars on an electric fire. Charlie still has the energy to slip past me and trot ahead, turning on the ridge and coming back to me. Bell lags behind. I count under my breath for no good reason. I try not to look back too much. Finally, there is a lull, a flattening before Heron Pike. I let my legs go ahead of me, loosen my body the way I was taught in Derbyshire when I first started fell running. I have tunnel vision. I have to remind myself to check in on the dogs, keep them in my attention.

In Ken Smith's strange, mesmerising urban poem 'Fox Running', we follow a creature that seems half animal and half man as he runs through the city of London at night. I read the piece first when I was in my early twenties – before that, I thought the only foxes in poems were archetypal figures, like the bold, definite creature that slunk into Ted Hughes's poem 'The Thought Fox', printing the page in its wake.[40] Fox was smouldering, certain and momentary. I had never read poetry like Ken Smith's before, work that seemed to escape from under my very eyes, that couldn't be pinned down. It reminded me of all the things I love about being able to set off running alone.

When we first encounter the unreliable narrator in Smith's

'Fox Running', he is already darting away from us, 'loose in his sleek skin'. That opening stanza puts the reader on the back foot. Fox is too lithe for his own body, too quick for himself. As we follow him 'into the tube maps / into the bus routes into the rails', he seems invisible and present at the same time, somewhere under the city's skin. He soon begins to shape-shift into a man, a lover, a runaway, a criminal. He can be both human and animal at the same time. Ken Smith's Fox is a paradox. He is 'running into his death / and his death always with him.'⁴¹

Even after he is apparently killed, he is still glimpsed: ghost fox, supernatural and bright, forever on the run. Towards the end of the poem, the yearning to see Fox merges with a yearning for language itself, a desire to find words for things that seem impossible to articulate.

I've always been enchanted by Smith's work and the promise of giving myself the slip somehow, of running out into oblivion. I think I run from the idea of being kept, the sense of being caught. In short, running gives me the illusion I might escape myself.

I gather pace along the ridge, seeing Fairfield and aiming for its bulk. There are more peaks and more miles to go after that, but for me its slopes are the zenith. Bell ranges and flits to my right. I'm exhilarated, fast and loose and free. Then, suddenly, I'm down, the stones beside the path rushing to meet me. I pick myself up too quickly, as if I can kid my body into thinking the fall never happened. I charge on, ignoring the new tenderness in my legs. When I glance down I'm surprised by the blood gushing from both knees, blood which surely can't be mine. But still I don't rest. As we find the descent from Fairfield's featureless top – a route that can be hard to find in poor visibility – and start to pick a way down towards Dove Crag and the Pikes, we pass a walker, up early to make the most of the day. She's middle-aged, clad in a raincoat and carrying trekking poles. Staring at my knees, she asks if I'm all right and if there's anything I need. I barely slow, nodding my breathless thanks to her.

It's always been hard for me to admit that I might have a problem with running. Since I was a teenager and used laps round the local football pitch to lose weight, to get rid of what I called 'puppy fat', I've seen it as a freedom and a source of strength. Recognising those times when competition becomes a burden, turns into sleepless nights, Ryvita biscuits for dinner, anger in front of the mirror, is difficult. I was brought up by two teachers and my mum always encouraged me to work hard at school, tidy my room, organise myself. When I discovered it aged twelve, the self-discipline of long-distance running seemed a fitting extension of that. And racing for the local athletics club created an environment where I could control myself and succeed, where what I put in was reflected in what I got out: the cross-country victories and the contented Saturday afternoons, the journey back on a bus that smelled of Deep Heat and strawberry laces. Through running, I could test myself, prove myself, show that I was capable. I could push past my pain threshold, being sick beside the track during rep sessions on Tuesday nights, sneaking out to swim. I remember reading about how famous decathlete Daley Thompson would train twice a day or more at Christmas, trying to get an edge over his rivals, and I vowed to do the same. I pored over athletics magazines and plotted ways to get faster, leaner, stronger – most of these involved eating in increasingly restrictive ways and running further each week, building up my mileage, doing hundreds of sit-ups in my room at night.

To me, addictions involved alcohol, drugs and fast food, not the almost-monastic discipline of running. When my concerned parents tried to get me to cut down as a fourteen-year-old, I was angry, seeing their interventions as intrusive, a way to stop me from being healthy and fulfilled. It was only later that I came to recognise my tendency to train hard as a symptom of controlling behaviour, began to connect it to times of my life when I wanted to punish myself somehow, exert order over chaos. Throughout my life, I've enjoyed the kind of relationship with running that you might have with an attractive but troubled partner. In my late teens, I competed obsessively on the track and on the churned-up fields of the cross-country circuit until injury pulled me up short. I was offered a sports scholarship to the USA which my damaged tendons prevented me from taking. Ever since then, I've had periods of jogging for pleasure punctuated by renewed bouts of competitiveness: becoming fit enough to join a club, starting to race again, beating myself up over my times and achievements, deciding to take a break. As a twenty-something, I cultivated an aptitude for marathon running and became preoccupied with faster and faster times, needing to be the quickest woman in my team. I eventually ran a sub-three-hour London marathon after a spell of punishing training: getting up at 4.30 a.m. to run long distances in the dark before work, head down through the winter darkness, quickening at the shadowy threat of strangers in cars. I loved and dreaded those solitary, almost dangerous mornings: once, I was sure I'd witnessed the aftermath of a robbery, a young man in a hooded top sprinting out of a garage in front of me into the maze of streets beyond, never glancing back. My marathon training also involved depriving myself of food, limiting myself to things I considered 'safe': avocados, apples, cucumber and fish.

There's something about the outwardness of running with dogs that lifts the veil of obsession. You have to adapt your pace to theirs, keep them with you, keep part of your mind with them at all times. As I stumble down towards Ambleside with my bloodied legs, I'm aware of Bell slowing and struggling. The path has been uneven on the way down, like the broken spine of a sheep, a skeleton to be picked and pored over. We've been weaving our way steadily. I remember I have a rucksack on, that I'm carrying water and energy bars. I slow, then I stop. The dogs trot faithfully back to me. I take the bottle out of my bag and pour some of the cool water into my hands, stoop to offer it to Bell and Charlie. They drink readily, greedily. Their mouths are gentle. It will see them right until we get to the beck where they can plunge into the water, drink and swim. I stroke the dogs. Then I take a swig from the bottle myself, another and another. I crouch down on the ground and splash my hurt knees with cool water.

When I get home, I open my notebook and I write a poem that has been burning in my head all the way along the ridges of the Fairfield Horseshoe. It says what I've always wanted to say about running and dogs.

**The Dogs**

Some mornings, waking up between the sandy whippet
and the black – their breathing slow as mine,
their eyes more sorrowful – I remind myself I'm not a dog.

It's not acceptable to taste the grass or roll in moss until
I'm musked with it. There are deer in the woods I'll never see.
My thirst discriminates. It does not have me bend

my grateful head to puddles, gutters, hollows
in the rock. I don't track rabbits in my sleep.
I'll not know love like theirs, observed in mute proximity,

and if I sometimes sit bolt upright after dark, sensing
a movement in the yard, it's only that I've learned
a little of their vigilance. I'm not like them:

one night I'll set off past the meadow, down
behind the beck, beyond the blunt profile of Silver Howe
and nobody will call me back.

When I'm finished, I close my book and I go and curl up in the
middle of the two dogs. Bell sighs contentedly. Outside, a static
rain has started to bead the glass. It's dark and we have nowhere
we need to go. Their breathing will lull me to sleep.

# Notes

1  Rainer Maria Rilke, 'Letter to N.N., 8 February 1912', *Rainer Maria Rilke: Selected Poems*, edited by Robert Vilain (Oxford University Press, 2001), p.296.

2  Helen Macdonald, *H is for Hawk* (Jonathan Cape, 2014).

3  Norman MacCaig, 'Landscape and I', *The Poems of Norman MacCaig*, edited by Ewan MacCaig (Polygon, 2005), p.286.

4  Norman MacCaig, 'On the Pier at Kinlochbervie', *The Poems of Norman MacCaig*, edited by Ewan MacCaig (Polygon, 2005), p.446.

5  Ibid.

6  Norman MacCaig, 'Heron', *The Poems of Norman MacCaig*, edited by Ewan MacCaig (Polygon, 2005), p.143.

7  Norman MacCaig, 'Goat', *The Poems of Norman MacCaig*, edited by Ewan MacCaig (Polygon, 2005), p.74.

8  Neil Levy, *Neuroethics: Challenges for the 21st Century* (Cambridge University Press, 2007), Kindle edition: 480.

9  Benjamin Myers, *Under the Rock: The Poetry of a Place* (Elliott & Thompson, 2018), p.48.

10  Anthony Hecht, 'A Hill', *Collected Earlier Poems* (Alfred A. Knopf, 2004), p.2.

11  W.A.B. Coolidge, *Alpine Studies* (Longmans, Green & Co, 1912), p.170.

12  Ibid.

13  Ibid., p.171.

14  Thomas Fletcher & Louise Platt, '(Just) a walk with the dog? Animal geographies and negotiating walking spaces', *Social & Cultural Geography*, Volume 19, Issue 2 (2016).

15  Ibid.

16  David Bell, *Derbyshire Ghosts & Legends* (Countryside Books, 1993), p.21.

17 The final version of 'The French for Death' was published in *Division Street* (Chatto & Windus, 2013).

18 From Barryland, Musée et Chiens du Saint-Bernard in Martigny.

19 Barbara Cratzius and Ursula Blancke, *Barry, The True Story of a Rescuer on Four Paws* (Bohem, 2015), p.1.

20 Seamus Heaney, 'The Tollund Man', www.poetryinternational.org/pi/poem/23607/auto/0/0/Seamus-Heaney/THE-TOLLUND-MAN/en/tile

21 Mike Arkus, 'Let Loose the Sled Dogs of War in the Depths of Greenland's Winter: Going Barmy instead of Balmy on the Looney Front (Part 5)', *Huffington Post*, 4 December 2015, updated 6 December 2017 (retrieved May 2020), www.huffpost.com/entry/let-loose-the-sled-dogs-o_b_6850496

22 Eileen Myles, *Afterglow: A Dog Memoir* (Grove Press, 2018), Kindle edition: 63.

23 Charles Foster, *Being a Beast* (Profile Books, 2016), p.20.

24 Ibid., p.30.

25 Derek Mahon, 'Leaves', *New Selected Poems* (The Gallery Press, 2016), p.23.

26 John Burnside, 'The Good Neighbour', *Selected Poems* (Jonathan Cape, 2006), p.100.

27 Maria Coffey, *Explorers of the Infinite: the secret spiritual lives of extreme athletes – and what they reveal about near-death experiences, psychic communication, and touching the beyond* (Jeremy P. Tarche/Penguin, 2008), Kindle edition: 65.

28 Ibid., Kindle edition: 72.

29 Angelique Chrisafis, 'French climber tells of ordeal on Pakistan's "Killer Mountain"', *The Guardian*, 1 February 2018 (retrieved May 2020), www.theguardian.com/world/2018/feb/01/french-climber-elisabeth-revol-describes-despairing-descent-on-pakistans-killer-mountain

30 Maria Coffey, *Explorers of the Infinite: the secret spiritual lives of extreme athletes – and what they reveal about near-death experiences, psychic communication, and touching the beyond* (Jeremy P. Tarche/Penguin, 2008), Kindle edition: 80.

31 Stephen Starr, 'On the Trail with Turkey's Wolf-Fighting Dogs', *Outside*, 16 February 2016 (retrieved May 2020), www.outsideonline.com/2052651/trail-turkeys-wolf-fighting-dogs

32  Elizabeth Bishop, 'One Art', www.poetryfoundation.org/
    poems/47536/one-art

33  Richard Wilbur, 'The Mind-Reader', in *Collected Poems 1943–2000*
    (Waywiser, 2005), p.207.

34  Jim Perrin, *Travels With The Flea and Other Eccentric Journeys*, second
    edition (Neil Wilson Publishing, 2003), postscript.

35  Mark Doty, *Dog Years: A Memoir* (Jonathan Cape, 2008), p.1.

36  Ibid., p.2.

37  Ibid., p.2.

38  Mariam Motamedi-Fraser, 'Dog words – or, How to think without
    language', *The Sociological Review*, Volume 67, Issue 2 (2019).

39  Mark Doty, *Dog Years: A Memoir* (Jonathan Cape, 2008), p.3.

40  Ted Hughes, 'The Thought Fox', in *Collected Poems* (Faber and Faber,
    2003), p.21.

41  Ken Smith, 'Fox Running', *Shed: Poems 1980–2001* (Bloodaxe Books,
    2002).

# Bibliography and further reading

Poetry

Bishop, Elizabeth, 'One Art', www.poetryfoundation.org/poems/47536/one-art

Burnside, John, 'The Good Neighbour', *Selected Poems* (Jonathan Cape, 2006).

Heaney, Seamus, 'The Tollund Man', www.poetryinternational.org/pi/poem/23607/auto/0/0/Seamus-Heaney/THE-TOLLUND-MAN/en/tile

Hecht, Anthony, 'A Hill', *Collected Earlier Poems* (Alfred A. Knopf, 2004).

Hughes, Ted, 'The Thought Fox', *Collected Poems* (Faber and Faber, 2003), p.21.

MacCaig, Norman, 'Goat', 'Heron', 'Landscape and I' and 'On the Pier at Kinlochbervie'. In *The Poems of Norman MacCaig*, edited by Ewan MacCaig (Polygon, 2005).

Mahon, Derek, 'Leaves', *New Selected Poems* (The Gallery Press, 2016).

Mort, Helen, 'The French for Death', *Division Street* (Chatto & Windus, 2013).

Rilke, Rainer Maria, 'Letter to N.N., 8 February 1912', *Rainer Maria Rilke: Selected Poems*, edited by Robert Vilain (Oxford University Press, 2001).

Smith, Ken, 'Fox Running', *Shed: Poems 1980–2001* (Bloodaxe Books, 2002).

Wilbur, Richard, 'The Mind-Reader', *Collected Poems 1943–2000* (Waywiser, 2005).


Other books

Alexis, André, *Fifteen Dogs: A Novel* (Serpent's Tail, 2015).

Bell, David, *Derbyshire Ghosts & Legends* (Countryside Books, 1993).

Coffey, Maria, *Explorers of the Infinite: the secret spiritual lives of extreme athletes – and what they reveal about near-death experiences, psychic communication, and touching the beyond* (Jeremy P. Tarche/Penguin, 2008).

Coolidge, W.A.B., *Alpine Studies* (Longmans, Green & Co, 1912).

Cratzius, Barbara and Blancke, Ursula, *Barry, The True Story of a Rescuer on Four Paws* (Bohem, 2015).

Doty, Mark, *Dog Years: A Memoir* (Jonathan Cape, 2008).

Foster, Charles, *Being a Beast* (Profile Books, 2016).

Goffman, Erving, *The Presentation of Self in Everyday Life* (Doubleday, 1959).

Levy, Neil, *Neuroethics: Challenges for the 21st Century* (Cambridge University Press, 2007).

Macdonald, Helen, *H is for Hawk* (Jonathan Cape, 2014).

Morley, Simon, *The Unfortunate Tourist of Helvellyn and His Faithful Dog* (Wordsworth Trust, 2003).

Myers, Benjamin, *Under the Rock: The Poetry of a Place* (Elliott & Thompson, 2018).

Myles, Eileen, *Afterglow: A Dog Memoir* (Grove Press, 2018).

Perrin, Jim, *Travels With The Flea and Other Eccentric Journeys*, second edition (Neil Wilson Publishing, 2003).

## Journals

Fletcher, Thomas & Platt, Louise, '(Just) a walk with the dog? Animal geographies and negotiating walking spaces'. In *Social & Cultural Geography*, Volume 19, Issue 2 (2016).

Motamedi-Fraser, Mariam. 'Dog words – or, How to think without language'. In *The Sociological Review*, Volume 67, Issue 2 (2019).

## Newspapers and magazines

Arkus, Mike, 'Let Loose the Sled Dogs of War in the Depths of Greenland's Winter: Going Barmy instead of Balmy on the Looney Front (Part 5)'. *Huffington Post*, 4 December 2015, updated 6 December 2017 (retrieved May 2020), www.huffpost.com/entry/let-loose-the-sled-dogs-o_b_6850496

Chrisafis, Angelique, 'French climber tells of ordeal on Pakistan's "Killer Mountain"'. *The Guardian*, 1 February 2018 (retrieved May 2020), www.theguardian.com/world/2018/feb/01/french-climber-elisabeth-revol-describes-despairing-descent-on-pakistans-killer-mountain

Starr, Stephen, 'On the Trail with Turkey's Wolf-Fighting Dogs'. *Outside*, 16 February 2016 (retrieved May 2020), www.outsideonline.com/2052651/trail-turkeys-wolf-fighting-dogs

## Television
*Wilderness Walks* (BBC, 1997–1998).

## Films
*When Dogs Fly* (Dean Potter, 2015).

## Websites
Barryland, the St Bernards Museum (Musée et Chiens du Saint-Bernard), Martigny: *www.barryland.ch*
Helen Mort: *www.helenmort.com*
Mountain Rescue (England and Wales): *www.mountain.rescue.org.uk*
Rachael Rodgers: *rachaelrodgersphotoworks.wordpress.com*
Search and Rescue Dog Association: *www.nsarda.org.uk*

# Acknowledgements

A big thank you to all at Vertebrate Publishing, especially Emma Lockley and Jon Barton.

Thanks to the editors of the *Journal of Performance Studies* where a version of the chapter #NeverLeaveTheDogBehind first appeared.

Thank you to Cedar Wright, Robert Macfarlane, Ed Douglas, Charles Foster, Mariam Motamedi-Fraser, Lucy Creamer, Chris Bonington, Rob Grange and everyone else at SARDA, Paul Besley and Scout, Jon Winter and Polly, Matthew Shipton, Maria Coffey, Jonathan Pitches, Jim Perrin, Heather Dawe, Mark Goodwin, Andrew Marshall, Helen Wakeford, Polly Atkin, Kathy Towers and all the other friends and authors whose wisdom found a way into this book, directly or indirectly. I'm very grateful for your time, your words and your trust. Thanks too to all the people on Twitter who were happy to send me photos of their dogs in the mountains!

Thank you to everyone at The Wordsworth Trust, especially Andrew Forster for his friendship, support and for allowing me to 'never leave the dog behind'. Thank you to Ambleside AC and everyone who kept me company on the fells as a climber and runner, particularly John Shedwick and Jan Bella.

Thanks to my husband Jess for his support, love and countless dog walks.

Thank you most of all to my parents, Andy and Janet, and my amazing gran Beryl for their patience and for nursing Bell and Charlie in their senior years, for welcoming dogs into the family. We didn't know we were dog lovers until we met Bell.

# About the Author

Helen Mort is a writer, trail runner and climber who lives in Sheffield. She teaches creative writing at Manchester Metropolitan University, and her published work includes poetry, fiction and non-fiction, with a particular interest in women and mountaineering. Her first poetry collection, *Division Street* (Chatto & Windus, 2013), was shortlisted for the Costa Prize and the T.S. Eliot Prize, and won the Fenton Aldeburgh First Collection Prize. In 2015, Helen was chosen as one of the Next Generation poets. Her first novel, *Black Car Burning* (Chatto & Windus, 2019), was longlisted for the Portico Prize and the Dylan Thomas Prize. Helen is the author of *Lake District Trail Running* (Vertebrate, 2016) and editor of *Waymaking* (Vertebrate, 2018); and she has written for *Alpinist*, *Climb*, *The Guardian*, *The Independent* and Radio 3. In 2017, she was a judge for the Man Booker International Prize and chair of judges for the Boardman Tasker Award for Mountain Literature. She was a judge for the 2019 Banff Mountain Book Prize. She has lived with a variety of dogs, but thinks a house is not a home without a whippet.